Dedicated to the special teachers in our lives who took time to share their love of literature with us, and to the teachers and the children of today who will share magical moments together.

BUILDING

ON

BOOKS

Integrating Children's Literature into the Curriculum

by
Kathy Faggella
Martha A. Hayes
Anne H. Leone

Art by
Kathy Faggella

FIRST TEACHER PRESS
First Teacher, Inc./Bridgeport, CT

ISBN 0-9615005-4-9

Library of Congress Catalog Card Number 86-82830

Design by Alice Cooke, Alice Cooke Design Associates, NY

Cover Design by Alice Cooke; Illustration by Debby Dixler

Edited by Lisa Lyons Durkin

Associate Editor: Francesca DeMaria

Editorial Assistant: Kathleen Hyson

Technical Advisor: Michael Bashar

Manufactured in the United States of America.

Published by First Teacher Press, First Teacher, Inc.
P.O. Box 29, 60 Main Street, Bridgeport, CT 06602.

Distributed by: Gryphon House, Inc.
                         P.O. Box 275
                         Mt. Ranier, MD 20712

TABLE OF CONTENTS

TABLE OF CONTENTS

COMMUNITY HELPERS

WE BELIEVE THAT

- children are never too young to enjoy storytime and that young children and well-chosen books belong together.
- children need good books to help extend their horizons as well as build skills and clarify concepts.
- children should be introduced to a wide variety of books to treasure. They should be encouraged to respond to them in as many ways as possible.
- children deserve to have books available to them in many different situations, presented in creative ways.
- children can increase their understanding of themselves and others as a result of being exposed to good books.
- children need a wealth of experiences with stories and books before the beginning of formal reading instruction.
- children need caring adults who will share a love of books, stories, poems, and rhymes with them.

OUR PHILOSOPHY

Young children begin to experience the beauty and rhythm of language when the first caring adult in their life speaks softly to comfort them. As children develop, they learn to respond to tone and cadence as nursery rhymes are chanted and simple tunes are sung or hummed.

"First books are meant to be explored fully."

Soon, children's eyes can focus on simple picture books held for them and before long, they are eager to hold those same sturdy "first" books. These books are meant to be held, tugged at, dropped, put in the mouth; it's part of the exploration pattern and a delightful part of development.

"Storytime is a special time for bonding."

We nurture this delight with books when we provide infants and toddlers not only with storytime every day, but also with board books of their own to "read" and to be read to them. Storytime becomes a special time for adults and children where bonding takes place and the children's interest in books gives them something to treasure and look forward to each day.

As children grow and their interest in books increases, they discover that books tell about many wonderful things, have beautiful pictures, and can be found in other places like schools, libraries, churches, stores, and even doctors' offices. Books open up new worlds and ideas that children are ready and eager to explore.

It is our role to keep this interest alive, to provide books and stories about many different things, to share old and new books, and to share our love of books.

"Well-chosen books are stepping stones to learning."

Well-chosen books can be used as stepping stones to lots of learning. If you think of books as bridges to anywhere and everywhere, you'll want to see how many you can find to fit into your curriculum. As you and the children explore new and old books and exciting ways to use them, you'll find that you use these "bridges" often and are beginning to look for new ones.

CONCEPTS AND SKILLS

**Children's Books and
Language Development**

Children's books promote language development in an interesting and enjoyable way. Storytime is a time for sharing together a love of books through listening and discussion. It is a "give and take" time when children can be helped to:
- understand new ideas that are presented.
- practice their listening skills.
- hear and use new words.
- have conversations about the story.
- ask and answer questions.
- write or scribble their own stories.

Visual Skills

Children's books help develop their visual skills. Colorful, interesting pictures tell a story they can follow with or without words. These books help children:
- focus their attention on the written word so that they realize that "writing is talk written down."
- follow the storyline as they look at the illustrations.
- develop the ability to read from left to right and from top to bottom.
- develop the ability to follow a sequence of events.
- respond to the beauty and color of the illustrations.

ABC, 123, Concepts

Children's books help present letters, numbers, and other concepts in interesting and unusual ways. They provide children with:
- pictures or illustrations to correspond with the letters, numbers, or concept being written about.
- opportunities to identify letters, numerals, and concepts shown.
- opportunities to learn new words and see new pictures.
- opportunities to practice and experiment with their new knowledge.
- opportunities to talk about and clarify their understanding of the letters, numbers, and concepts.

Children's books are keys to learning about many wonderful things. We are the ones who will help the children in our care use these keys.

STORYTELLING

"The telling of stories is a wonderful way to entertain children."

Storytelling is one of the oldest forms of entertainment. It's been around for thousands of years, long before books were even thought of. Surely the telling of stories is a wonderful way to bring entertainment to children. Plus, stories are rich in new concepts, ideas, and vocabulary; many of them also give children a change to participate in the music of language.

Storytelling a is a very personal experience for the young child and, just think, there is no book to get in the way. Each child who is being told a story often experiences a sense of bonding with the teller, as well as with others in the group. The storyteller reads the child's face and communication is established on a very special level.

"Tell personal stories and folktales with lots of repetition."

Since you, the teacher, are such a central figure in the children's lives, it's important that you share your storytelling talents with them. They'll feel really special if you make the time and effort to do this for them. Start by telling them little personal stories about your family, pets, and things you've done. You know how they love to learn more about their teacher, so you'll have a captive audience. Move on to simple stories with lots of repetition—folktales are great. Here are some suggestions:

- The Three Bears
- The Three Billy Goats Gruff
- Ask Mr. Bear
- Mr. Rabbit and the Lovely Present
- Akimba and the Magic Cow
- Topingey
- Tikki Tikki Tembo
- The Five Chinese Brothers

"Investigate storytelling programs at your local library."

Investigate the cultural backgrounds of the children in your care and see if you can find some good stories to tell that reflect these backgrounds. Encourage parents and grandparents to come in and tell stories; in some cultures, storytelling is still a popular pastime. You also should find out about storytelling programs in your local children's library and get involved.

Happily for all of us, there has been a recent rebirth of interest in storytelling. Some local school systems have storytelling contests and programs where older children compete and the winners are chosen to tell stories in various locations. There is a National Society for the Preservation and Protection of Storytelling (NAPPS); unique storytelling groups are springing up in many areas. Most of the smaller groups meet on a regular basis to practice telling and listening to stories and they encourage new members. Many of the members like to be invited to share their talents with children in school situations. Consult your local newspapers and libraries for further information about storytelling groups in your community.

"Children can be the storytellers, too."

After all this exposure to storytelling, children should be ready and anxious to tell their own stories. Here are some suggestions to start them on:

■ Encourage children to tell stories to each other in small groups.

■ Work on the fact that stories should be short and that they have a beginning, a middle, and an end. (Often, children don't know when to stop.)

■ Start a story and have children fill in the blanks. *"One in the dark woods, there was a _____ and _____ met a _____ and it said, "If you do _____ _____ _____ , I'll give you a magical _____ ."*

■ Take a story with dialogue, hand out one end of several colored strands of yarn to several children and when you want these children to participate, you pull on the other end of the yarn.

■ Try using simple props or nonfrightening masks, especially with shy children.

After children have worked with small groups over a period of time, they may be ready to move on to a larger group, still in their own secure setting. If so, this is the time to encourage them to speak out and perhaps even to dramatize their stories.

Storytelling, besides being very entertaining, can be the foundation for learning more about your children, their backgrounds and interests.
It can open up a whole new world of experiences for everyone involved. Enjoy!

"Use simple props with shy children."

"Storytelling is a foundation for learning."

HOW TO USE THIS BOOK

"Build bridges from books to all areas of your curriculum."

Building on Books will show ways to use books and children's literature to build all types of bridges for the young children you teach. The book chapters have been divided by themes and curriculum areas. Experience shows that most curriculum for young children is thematic, so this book has been divided into subjects, such as "All About Me," "Seasons," "Words," "Colors," "Poetry and Rhymes," "Community Helpers," and so on. This will enable you to easily fit the material into your existing program.

"Introduce new books at circletime and in your library corner."

Each chapter contains a short description of between seven and twelve books that will enhance children's understanding or enjoyment of a particular subject. For each book listed under *Stories for Circletime*, there are two group activities that can be used during or after the reading of the story. Books that you might want to reserve for book corner use can be found in *In the Library Corner*. The way that you introduce or use these books will depend upon your group. You may wish to give a short introduction to a book, read it in its entirety, or just place it in the library corner and let children explore it on their own.

In each chapter, you will find discussions of the types of books you might want to include in your library corner and some suggested general "motivators" you can use to encourage children to explore the books. These questions and directives fit not only the suggested books but also others that deal with the same themes.

"Plan projects to extend books beyond reading."

Involvement with books and the library corner should extend beyond "reading," so each chapter also includes three or more project pages that list, step-by-step, hands-on activities related to books to do with children. Through these projects, children will extend their enjoyment or interest in the themes and the books. They will learn about bookmaking, including the importance of art in literature. In each chapter, they will have the opportunity to take part in making the library corner a more enticing or cozy place.

On the project pages, the directions given refer to a child. We use the term "adult" when a certain task is too difficult or too dangerous for a young child to do alone. However, you must be the final judge of what your children can do. Remember that safety is always the major concern.

Use the suggestions in *Building on Books* as bridges to the learning of concepts and skills. You will want to personalize the books and the situations according to individuals, your group, and the facilities and literature available to you. Use this book as a guide to assist you in finding books and in planning related experiences. Above all, use it to help you develop in your children a love of books and literature.

GETTING READY

YOUR LIBRARY AREA

"A good library corner can be your best teaching tool."

A good library corner can be your best teaching tool. It can provide the resources necessary for just about any activity, while providing space for children to explore and relax.

A library corner is much more than shelves of books and resources. It is a total environment that conveys a special atmosphere and should be well used and enjoyed by both the teachers and the children.

You, as the teacher, will be the one to set the tone for the use of your library corner. Children will notice if your corner is a vital part of the whole classroom every day or if it is just a time-filling place.

Here are some hints for making the book corner a real teaching tool for you and a learning tool for the children.

"Make sure you have a well-stocked library."

First, make sure you have a well-stocked library. Young children enjoy a great variety of children's literature and appreciate having the opportunity to make choices as to the books they will read. (See the following pages for suggestions about the types of books to include and how to acquire them.)

"Systematically introduce new books."

Second, systematically introduce new books.

■ Read one during each storytime period and place it into the library corner.

■ Give one to a child, if you think he has a particular interest in the theme or type of characters.

■ Pull out all the books by one author or illustrator, or all the books on one particular theme or holiday and display them, discussing the fact that there is a connection between the books.

■ Intrigue the children by starting a book but deliberately not finishing it. Then, leave it out in the library corner for the curious.

■ Bring in one prop to introduce a book you will read. Let children guess how it will fit into the story.

■ Encourage a small group of children to pick two or three books, find a comfortable spot, and read silently for three or four minutes. (You may have to read a book aloud if a child becomes very enthusiastic about one of his selections.)

"Follow up a child's reading."

Third, make sure to follow up a child's reading.

■ Observe what each child is reading and suggest a follow-up activity to do.

■ Suggest another book similar to one the child loved.

■ Let the child share a favorite book with a small group of children, if he really shows enthusiasm for it. He could tell the story and show the pictures or his original drawings.

"Make sure the library is used—not abused."

Fourth, make sure the library corner is used, but not abused.

■ Set limits on the number of children in the area and on the acceptable type of behavior. (Use a tag hung on yarn to admit children to the area, if necessary. For example, set out six tags if you allow six children in at one time. Each child wears a tag while in the corner. Or, make a rule that all children must have a seat to sit on.)

■ Have a child help with the librarian duties, such as checking to make sure all books are put back on the shelves in the proper color-coded areas or having the child help with display set-ups. Your child librarians can make sure books are properly handled. They may even be able to take care of any type of checkout system you have.

"Keep the library current."

Fifth, keep the library corner current by using it.

■ You can do this by grabbing every opportunity to use the library as a resource. You can pull out the book on dinosaurs when a child brings in his beloved plastic dinosaur figures. Use the resources to teach information based on a child's interests.

■ Enlist children to help you change displays. (Pick a new child each week—it will be a special time spent with you.)

■ Plan one new group activity to be done inside the library corner space each week.

Remember, you are the best role model for the children. If you make the library corner inviting, special, and relaxing, and, if you really use it, the children will, too.

THINGS TO INCLUDE IN A LIBRARY CORNER

"Variety is the key to choosing books for the library corner."

A good library corner should have a large selection of various types of books and other multi-media materials for children and teachers to use. The suggestions following are for the ideal library corner. Do not be discouraged if yours is only a very modest version of the one described. Just plan to add on to the library corner when funds and donations come your way and you'll be surprised what can happen in a few years!

Variety is the key word for choosing books for your library. An ideal one would have a large selection of each of the following types of books. However, you can start small and make sure you have a couple of each.

Storybooks

From classics like Gag's *Millions of Cats* to current favorites like Sesame Street's *The Monster at the End of this Book*, include your favorite read-alouds as well as wordless books.

Poetry Books

From "Mother Goose" rhymes to "Madeline" verse stories to poems by Robert Louis Stevenson, be sure to include at least a few books.

Concept Books

Include alphabet books, number books, books about opposites, animals, transportation, and families.

Sense Books

Include the "scratch and sniff", the "touch" books (like *Pat the Bunny*), and tiny "nutshell-type" books. There are now even books that have music boxes inside and computer chips that play a song or allow a child to play on a keyboard!

Beginning Readers

Have these for the very few exceptional children who have learned to read very early. The Dr. Seuss books are perennial favorites.

Reference Books

These are to be used as resources by you with the children. They might include *Childcraft, Compton's PreEncyclopedia,* or *Young Readers Press' First*

Dictionary. Also, include a few books that children can use alone such as picture books of dinosaurs, eggs, snakes, fish, and so on.

Books by the Same Author

Include a set of books by one author so that you can do an author study. For example, find as many of Robert McCloskey's books as you can, or those by Ezra Jack Keats or Eric Carle. Talk about style, format, and content. Children ARE interested in who wrote the book or who drew the pictures!

Child-Authored Books

Place books written by your children in a special space so they can be shared with everyone. Encourage children to write their own books and read others written by their classmates. Whenever possible, type their stories or dialogues into their books.

MULTI-MEDIA MATERIALS

"Library corners should contain more than books."

While books are still the core of your library corner, we now have other things to add to it. The ideal corner will have some of each of the following. The major drawback is that most of this equipment is expensive. However, you can plan fundraisers to help bring in money for these extra items. Careful planning over the years will let you build a beautifully complete library corner.

Audio-Tapes

Children enjoy "reading" along in storybooks, as they listen to a tape of the story. You will need a tape recorder and individual headphones. (You can order these tapes through catalogues or find them in bookstores and record shops.)

Video Tapes

There are many tapes out for young children from Disney favorites to the Muppets to Faery Tale Theatre. Most of these are for sheer entertainment. (You will need a videotape machine which you can rent or purchase. If you have a machine, you might borrow tapes from the parents.)

Records

Records have been around for a long time and still offer good music, activity games, and stories for children. Early Childhood supply catalogues offer a good variety, as do some of the larger record stores.

Children's Magazines

There are a few magazines for young children. They often contain activities to be done in the book or cut out of the magazine. These would include the *"Sesame Street"* type of magazine. *"Ranger Rick"* and National Geographic's *"World"* are for older children, but have magnificent photos and illustrations in them.

Picture File

To complete the multi-media materials in the library corner, add a picture file and games or activities to go along with the books. A picture file can be as simple as file folders with categories of pictures such as animals, flowers, children, or toys. Children can help cut out more magazine pictures, catalogue pictures, and old textbook pictures to add to the file.

Use these pictures for making games, for making scrapbooks, or as pictures to encourage storytelling by the children. Use them in displays and as rewards or prizes to be given to the children.

THE PHYSICAL SPACE

A library corner should not only be well-equipped with books and multi-media materials; it should be inviting, comfortable, quiet most times, apart from the flow of most traffic (but not from the teacher's eyes), and well lit. A library corner should beckon children to come in and stay a while. It should be a clearly defined area that is special. It should contain sturdy shelves for books, tapes, and records. Cabinets can house tape recorders and phonographs. A table in the center is good for doing activities.

"Your library corner should be inviting."

Cushions, set around the edge of the corner, make it more comfortable for those who love sitting on the floor. You also might consider constructing a unique seating place from large cardboard boxes or wood or papier-mache in the shape of a boat, rocketship, barn, jungle, castle, hollow tree, airplane, circus tent, train, or underwater submarine.

Something as simple as streamers hung from a central point on the ceiling and trailing down into a circle around the edges of the corner can create a circus tent effect. Children can sit in individual circus train "boxcars" with paper plate wheels pasted on and "read" their books.

Taking the time to make a papier-mache rock is well worth the effort. It is like bringing the outside indoors. Children love to sit on and around the rock and "read" and look at books. A large real or artificial tree branch would be another outside touch. These add to the inviting atmosphere that should pervade the library corner.

Each library can contain other special spots. All you need is a corner and you can have a beauty spot, a nursery rhyme or poetry corner, a book-making center, and an art area.

Beauty Spot

The beauty spot is one place where you can let your artistic and creative spirit free. This spot is a lovely, sometimes elegant, place where you show off fresh flowers, ceramic figurines, candles, fruit-filled baskets, special collections, and lacy tablecloths. Let children help you make the arrangements. Children do appreciate seeing beautiful items set out in an attractive manner. Place objects on a side table or shelf. It should be out of the way of any accidental bumping. If you have a glass case, use that for little collections. Children may also want to contribute to the beauty spot. But, change the beauty spot frequently; even beauty can be tiring if left out too long!

Nursery Rhyme Corner

A Nursery Rhyme corner can be used to highlight one nursery rhyme each week, complete with illustrations. Place a picture and its rhyme inside a frame that is hung permanently in one corner of the library area. This frame can be a purchased, clear acrylic type or a homemade, fabric frame covered with a gay, colored print. Cut, draw, or trace an illustration. Either use a primary typewriter to print out the nursery rhyme or print it by hand on experience chart paper.

Each week, recite a new rhyme, show the illustration, and use this corner to invite children into nursery rhyme-related activities.

Book-Making Center

A book-making center should be part of every library area. It should be located slightly apart from the shelves of books, but still be a part of the whole area. Even the youngest of children love to make little books that are all their own. Encourage them to be young authors by having a few simple materials available at all times in this corner.

You'll Need:

• a few blank books (Include tiny, tall, foldouts, giant, oblong, and other simple shapes; made with newsprint and cardboard and either sewn or stapled together.)

• marking pens and crayons

• colored paper

• scissors

• glue

• plastic bins for storing everything

Place blank books on shelves and pens, crayons, colored paper, and scissors in the bins. Children can compose their own little books and draw pictures in the blank books.

Art Area

An art area nearby or in the library corner can encourage children to draw their own interpretations of stories they hear or read. Keep materials—markers, crayons, paints, paper—in a caddy to be replaced on the shelf when art is completed.

RUNNING THE LIBRARY

Having a well-stocked library corner is just the beginning. You also need to work out the mechanics of running it. Through experience, you will find out what works best for your own situation. Here, however, are some ideas to consider.

Color Code Books

Color code each book for easy replacement on shelves. Place a small colored dot on the bottom part of the spine to coordinate with a specific area in the library corner.

You may want only to divide your library corner into a few categories at first. Color code storybooks, children's handwritten books, reference books, tapes, and records. Place a dot or paper strip on the shelf to indicate where each kind of book is to be placed. Alphabetizing at this point in time will only be of use to you—not to the children. (Actually, this type of sorting would be frustrating for you since you would have to help put the books away.)

Check-out Policies

Make a policy about whether books may be taken out of the library corner or not. You may run the risk of losing a few if you allow children to bring books home. Yet, children often love to share books with their parents.

If you decide to allow books to be taken home, you might want to consider these three suggestions:

■ The simplest suggestion is to have a sign-out sheet for children or parents to sign when they take out the books.

■ Make a large size (6" x 8") library card for each child. Keep all cards in a box on the library corner table. When a child decides to take a book home, he sets it aside until an adult (teacher or parent) writes the title of the book on his library card.

■ If you want to be very organized, you may want to glue a library pocket inside the front or back cover of each book. Place a card with the title and author in the envelope. When a child wants to take the book home, remove the card from the book, let the child sign it, and keep it in a file on the library corner table.

AND, if you are still having a difficult time getting books back to your library corner, set out an amnesty box near the door so parents cannot help but notice it!

OBTAINING BOOKS

Here are some suggestions for acquiring books for your library corner, including accepting all donations you are given. You can then go through them and, using the suggested guidelines below, choose the ones worth keeping.

Creative Ways to Obtain Books

■ First, you can always borrow books from the public library. Most of these allow teachers to borrow large numbers of picture books and sign them out for a month at a time. Check your local library.

■ Go to local public library sales. These usually occur once a year. Children's books can be purchased for under a dollar quite often.

■ Go to tag, yard, or garage sales and buy children's books.

■ Accept donations from children in your school. Let parents know that whenever they want to get rid of books, you'll accept them.

■ Encourage parents to come in to share a book with children and leave it as a donation. Place a nameplate in it, of course, and write a thank you note. This is particularly great for each child's birthday. The parent can read the book to the class on the child's birthday and then give it as a present to the school!

■ Bring in your own books. You may want to set aside a special, ever-changing, shelf just for these.

■ Go through used bookstores and buy some there.

Guidelines for Choosing Good Books

Not everything printed for children is good children's literature. While we hope to choose good literature, we can also accept the fact that some books are still enjoyable for just the moment. It is fine that a library corner has both types of books. It is important that a child enjoys a book. How many times have we cringed at books with nonsense rhymes only to realize that children adored them! So find out which books children love and include these.

Here is a list of suggested guidelines to help you sort out the better books—those you will want to have permanently. Look at the book, read it, and answer these questions about it.

■ Does the book have a good theme? The theme of the book should reflect the needs and interests of the children. Good themes make good, interesting plots for picture books.

Preschool children have short attention spans; therefore, books should be short and, if possible, participatory. Children love to name things and point to objects in the books.

Young children are egocentric so many picture books deal with themes about that age children and the problems and concerns they have in growing up. Preschoolers are curious and enjoy stories about everyday experiences and people like themselves. They like books that show their beginning sense of independence and their budding ability to make value judgments.

■ Does the book have memorable characters? Children want characters that are believable and with whom they can relate. Those characters need not be human ones, but the fantasy characters must show human traits for the children to be able to relate to them.

■ Does the book have illustrations that are attractive, artistic, and go with the text? Young children are very literal and will notice when the illustrations do no accurately interpret the text or when they are out of order.

■ Does the book fit the young child in physical size, format, and binding? Most good books for children are small enough for them to hold alone and have only a few words on each page with large type that attracts even the nonreader's eyes. Bindings must be sturdy enough for the young reader's lifestyle with books.

ALL
ABOUT ME

ALL ABOUT ME

Children at this stage are occupied with the many ways in which they're growing and changing. They're curious; they're striving to achieve competence in many areas; and they need to be assured that everything is okay. We can use books to help us discuss characters who are very much like the children in our care. Books and suggestions like the ones below will help you get to know your children better.

Happy to Be Me
Bobbie Kalman

Divided into topics such as "Happy to Be Me," "I Was a Baby Once," and "Changing As I Grow," this book has bright, detailed pictures plus questions to ask about each illustration.
■ You may wish to examine each page separately so that children have time to recall and discuss when they were involved in similar situations.
■ Each day, choose a small circle of children. Ask each child in the group to make one positive statement about the next child, such as, "I like Mary's smile" or "I like the way Tyrone does _____."

Someday with My Father
Helen E. Buckley

A little girl daydreams about someday skiing, fishing, sailing, and hiking with her dad. Unfortunately, she has to wait until the cast is off her leg so she has to settle for a warm, loving dad reading to her.
■ Talk about wishing. Build on sports activities in the book for movement exercises—stretching, casting for fish, throwing a rope, striding, make-believe skiing. ("I wish I could ski.")
■ Have children role play having a cast on either their foot, hand, or arm. Ask them to show what they can and cannot do while making believe that particular limb is not able to be used. This may provide discussions of empathy for others—including the handicapped.

The Growing Story
Ruth Krauss

Some chicks, a puppy, and a boy are just beginning to grow. The boy is upset because he's not growing as quickly as the chicks, puppy, and even some flowers.
■ Discuss growth patterns in animals, plants, and people. Talk about things children can do now that they couldn't do as babies.
■ See if children can arrange themselves into groups in which they are exactly the same height. Then, talk about differences in height, using terms like *taller, tallest, shorter, shortest*. After that, have them try standing in groups of three showing three differences in height.

I'm in Charge
Joan Drescher

Father's upstairs working on a typewriter and Mother's away at work; Marshall is in charge and is to call Dad only in an emergency.
■ Discuss the things that happened in the story. Ask if Marshall should have made himself a snack or allowed his friends to visit. Then, have children tell what they would have done if they had been Marshall.
■ Set up several situations in the housekeeping corner that follow the story line. Have children role play, changing parts frequently.

A STORY ABOUT ME

One day I said that I did not want to be a little
_____ anymore. I did not want to play with my
best friends _____ and _____ anymore. I
did not want to live at _____
anymore. So I set out to see who else I could be!

First, I saw a bird up in a tree.
"Hello, my name is _____ and I want to
be a bird like you." But the bird flew away.
I couldn't follow because I couldn't fly.

Next I saw a squirrel under a tree.
"Hello, my name is _____ and I
want to be a squirrel like you." But the squirrel
ran up the tree. I tried to follow, but I couldn't climb
that high.

Just then I saw a gopher.
"Hello, my name is _____ and
I want to be a gopher like you." But the
gopher dug a hole in the ground and disappeared.
I tried to follow him but couldn't fit down the hole.

Then I saw a frog sitting on a rock.
"Hello, my name is _____ and I
want to be a frog just like you." But the frog
jumped into the brook and swam away. I was
going to jump, too, but I decided I didn't want to.

"I can't be a very good bird, or a squirrel,
or a gopher or a frog, but...
I can still be a little _____.
I can ride my _____.
I can read my favorite book _____.
I can eat _____.
I can sing my favorite song, _____.
And I can hug my _____.
       I LIKE BEING ME!

ALL ABOUT ME

You might want to introduce any or all of the following books during group circletime. Then, you can place them in the library corner so that children can explore the books on their own.

Fun with My Friend
Bobbie Kalman

This book talks about friends and the many different things they can do together.

Can I Help?
Anne and Harlow Rockwell

Sometimes this little girl's parents say, "no" when she wants to help or do things by herself. This is a good book to stimulate discussions about waiting to do a task until a child is more grown-up.

I Can Take a Walk!
Shigeo Watanabe

A wonderful bear slips through a fence and climbs a little mound he calls a mountain. He does only one thing but embroiders on the truth when telling about his walk. Children will delight in finding out what he REALLY does and in guessing what he actually says in this wordless book.

When I have a Little Girl
and
When I have a Little Boy
Charlotte Zolotow

These two books talk about things that children would like to do but that grown-ups won't let them do. They will have fun making comparisons.

My Mom Travels a Lot
Caroline Feller Bauer

Good and bad things happen when Mom is away. (Susie, the dog, has a surprise in this story!) A good story for discussion time.

Katy's First Haircut
Gibbs Davis

Everybody wonders what it's like to get a first haircut. The pictures help show how Katy felt and children will enjoy talking about her emotions.

MOTIVATORS

Try some of these motivators to encourage children to explore books in you library corner. They will fit one or more of the books above and other books that you have collected that deal with the theme of "All About Me."

1. Find a book that shows children doing some activity that you like to do.
2. Will you find a book with pictures that show what we looked like when we were babies?
3. Find a book that shows brothers and sisters and one that shows pictures of children and their friends.
4. Find a book that shows some boys and girls doing jobs around the house to help the family.
5. Bring your favorite book over and tell us about it.
6. Find a book showing parents and children doing things together.
7. Is there a book with a child that looks like you?

SEE HOW WE GROW!

YOU'LL NEED:

 colored construction paper    ribbon   photos   masking tape   scissors

WHAT TO DO:

1. Cut a piece of ribbon the exact height of each child in class.

Tape ribbons to wall starting at the floor and running straight up about 5" from each other.

2. A colored construction paper flower is cut out and taped to the top of the ribbon and a photo of the child is placed inside the flower center.

3. Label the wall, "See How We Grow." Discuss the concepts of taller, tallest and shorter, shortest. Compare heights. Remeasure half way through year and end of year. Make the flower grow.

birthday party book

YOU'LL NEED:

construction paper   plain paper

real birthday candles (or paper ones)

markers

glitter and glue

metal rings   scissors

WHAT TO DO:

1. Adult cuts out two colored construction paper birthday cake shapes. Child decorates with marker, glitter.

2. Adult cuts out six pieces of plain paper in same birthday cake shape. These pages are attached with decorated covers by two metal rings.

3. At beginning of school year, child glues on candles that correspond to present age. Pages are blank.

4. "Birthday Cake Books" are displayed on bulletin board with calendar of children's birthdays.

5. When each child celebrates his/her birthday during the year, child adds another candle to the birthday cake book.

6. The pages are used to draw illustrations of the birthday celebration and signatures of classmates. Book then goes home with child.

ALL ABOUT ME

GOOD MORNING SCHOOL I'M SLEEPY I'M HUNGRY PLAYTIME T.V. Time

YOU'LL NEED:

24" long by 6" tall piece of paper
(can be taped together)

stamp pad

crayons

fine tipped black marker

WHAT TO DO:

1. Adult folds strip of paper into six parts. Each 'page' measures 4" x 6". First page is cover. Write title on cover. Child can illustrate cover.

press

print

marker

2. Child makes thumb prints on each page to show him/herself and others in family or friends.

3. Adult or child can add eyes, mouth, arms and legs, as well as clothes to make thumb prints look like child and friends. Use marker.

4. Child draws in background for each page. Encourage child to follow sequence of his or her day. Draw a few clocks, also.

5. Refold the book and let the child open each page and "read" the story of his day.

BIBLIOGRAPHY

Bauer, Caroline Feller. *My Mom Travels a Lot.* Frederick Warne, 1981.

Binzen, Bill. *First Day in School.* Doubleday, 1972.

Bruna, Dick. *When I'm Big.* Methuen, 1981.

Buckley, Helen E. *Someday with My Father.* Harper & Row, 1985.

Caines, Jeannette. *Just Us Women.* Harper & Row, 1982.

Davis, Gibbs. *Katy's First Haircut.* Houghton, Mifflin, 1985.

Drescher, Joan. *I'm in Charge.* Little, Brown, 1981.

Ets, Marie Hall. *Just Me.* Viking, 1965.

Fitzhugh, Louise. *I Am Five.* Delacorte, 1978.

————. *I Am Four.* Delacorte, 1982.

————. *I Am Three.* Delcorte, 1982.

Holzenthaler, Jean. *My Hands Can.* E. P. Dutton, 1978.

Hopkins, Lee Bennett, comp. *By Myself.* Thomas Y. Crowell, 1980.

Iverson, Genie. *I Want to Be Big.* E. P. Dutton, 1979.

Kalman, Bobbie. *Fun with My Friend.* Crabtree, 1985.

————. *Happy to Be Me.* Crabtree, 1985.

Keats, Ezra Jack. *Whistle for Willie.* Viking, 1964.

Krauss, Ruth. *The Growing Story.* Harper & Row, 1947.

Lloyd, Errol. *Nandy's Bedtime.* Merrimack, 1983.

Moncure, Jane Belk. *Now I Am Three!* Children's Press, 1984.

Oxenburg, Helen. *First Day of School.* Dial Books, 1983.

Rockwell, Anne and Harlow. *Can I Help?* Macmillan, 1982.

Rubel, Nicole. *Me and My Kitty.* Macmillan, 1983.

Watanabe, Shigeo. *I Can Take a Walk!* G. P. Putnam, 1984.

Zolotow, Charlotte. *When I Have a Little Girl.* Harper & Row, 1984.

————. *When I Have a Son.* Harper & Row, 1967.

THE
SEASONS

FALL

Fall is a time to say goodbye to the hot lazy days of summer and hello to crisp autumn weather. Sometimes, the warm weather doesn't seem to want to leave, just as we and the children are reluctant to leave vacations behind and begin new tasks. The books and activities listed below will provide a springboard for discussing the changing seasons.

I Like Weather
Aileen Fisher

This is a lovely book of poetry for all seasons. Children will enjoy the images the words make as well as the actual illustrations.

■ You might introduce the topic of changing seasons by reading "I like summer but when it's fall nothing is better at all, at all." Children can talk about outdoor fall activities they enjoy.

■ Read "Weather is full of the nicest sounds." Assign a line to each child after writing each of them on a piece of oaktag for visual reinforcement. The lines are short and children will respond to the sounds and learn them quickly. Put the poem together a line at a time when children are familiar with it and then tape record the children's choral reading. Later, talk about weather changes and sounds.

The Fall of Freddie the Leaf
Leo Buscaglia

This gentle story of the life and death of Freddie the leaf will help children understand the changing seasons and also life cycles.

■ Discuss changes that occur in nature in the fall. Use the book's illustrations to help children understand what happens to leaves and notice other changes in nature and in themselves.

■ Take children on a "listening" and "seeing" walk. Discuss differences in fall and summer sights and sounds. Collect signs of fall for the nature corner and future art activities.

Frederick
Leo Lionni

Frederick is a tiny mouse whose brothers and sisters are busily gathering food as they prepare for winter. Frederick, however, prepares in other ways—he is collecting words.

■ Reread the book with children and discuss ways in which animals and people prepare for winter and ways in which the children themselves will help get ready for winter. Talk about the words Frederick collects.

■ Make several paper plate, mouse-face stick puppets. Choose four or five children to be mice. Have them tell ways they would get ready for winter. Ask them to use their favorite words about fall.

The All-Around Pumpkin Book
Margery Cuyler

This book is chock full of information about growing pumpkins and using them in recipes and crafts. It also tells about how Jack-o'-lanterns began.

■ Bring in pumpkins of various sizes and shapes. Discuss color, texture, size, shape, and how they grow.

■ Cut one pumpkin open. Help children examine the seeds, choose some to save for planting, clean others off, and roast the cleaned ones for eating at snacktime.

FALL POEMS

Discuss the season of fall with children. After experiencing some of the changes that happen outside in the fall, suggest writing a class poem. Use one of these forms and tell children exactly what is needed in each line.

CINQUAIN

noun : Fall
two adjectives : Nippy, Blustery
3 "ing" verbs : Whirling, Swirling, Twirling
a thought : Bright colored leaves float on the wind.
a synonym for noun in line 1 : Autumn

HAIKU

Apple, pumpkins, grapes, (5 syllables)
Harvest foods for us to eat (7 ")
Fall sweetly gives all. (5 ")

(17 syllables that suggest an aspect of nature)

FIVE SENSES

Fall is orange and red
It tastes like pumpkins and apples
It sounds like old, crumbled newspapers
It smells like hot, cinnamon-y cider steaming
It looks like a beautiful, gypsy coat
It makes me feel like running and yelling.

CONCRETE

Fall means we make jack-o-lanterns from pumpkins and eat the...
seeds seeds seeds seeds seeds seeds seeds seeds

Fall means that Dad and I get to go at to football games. Yeh!

Fall means we go to the apple orchard and pick bags of apples right off the trees! apple apple apple apple apple

NAME

Feathers dropped from birds flying south
Animals get ready for winter
Leaves all over the ground
Lovely time of the year

WINTER

Winter's coming—sometimes with glorious clear days for outside play; sometimes with sleety, slushy days meant for indoor activities. The following books and suggestions will help you capture the magic of winter and nourish in children wonder and appreciation of well-chosen books.

In the Flaky Frosty Morning
Karla Kuskin

This little book begins "In the flaky, frosty morning some mittens made a start," and ends "I dwindle, droop, the sun will set on snowman soup." The text has a singing quality children will want to hear often.

■ Talk about the life cycle of a snowman. Discuss the pinks, whites, and blues of the illustrations. Plan your own snowman pictures or bulletin boards. (A pink and blue tissue paper snowman and snowflakes on a white background produce a charming effect.)

■ If you're lucky enough to have snow that's good for building snowmen, do it. Read the book first, then see if you and the children can follow all the steps in the poem, ending by making your unique snowperson.

Animals in Winter
Henrietta Bancroft and Richard G. Van Gelder

One of the Let's-Read-and-Find-Out Science Books, this easy-to-read, informative book has lifelike pictures of birds and small animals for children to look at. It talks about the different ways that animals and birds get ready for winter.

■ Discuss hibernation and migration. List the animals who "rest" for the winter on an experience chart and add pictures. Talk about birds who leave us to go to warmer places. List names and add pictures. Talk about animals who store up extra food for the winter and animals who grow thicker coats. Discuss how people get ready for winter.

■ Set up a feeding spot for squirrels and birds. Develop a system for keeping track of who is responsible for feeding the birds, what and how much each type of bird eats, and how many different kinds of birds are seen. Have other children leave food for the squirrels. When it snows, help children observe the tracks.

Happy Winter
Karen Gundersheimer

This charming rhyming text tells about the wonderful winter things two little sisters do all day long. They do all kinds of things inside and outside including sledding, writing on the snow, playing dress-up indoors on a cold, sleety day, reading, taking hot baths, and finally snuggling into bed with Mother singing a winter lullaby.

■ Talk about things we can do outside in the winter that we can't do at any other time. Ask children to brainstorm some outside winter words.

■ Put them up on a winter tree or bulletin board along with some winter pictures. Some good words to use as starters are *snow (slushy, slippery, sifting, softly); wind (blowing, biting, stinging);* and so on.

■ Discuss things you can do inside in the winter when it's too nasty to go outside. Try special dress-ups, sing-alongs, making presents for special grownups, or making a new snack. You may wish to try the delicious recipe for fudge cake in *Happy Winter*.

Snowmen All Around

⭐ FINGERPAINT SNOWMEN

Beat with a mixer:
½ cup laundry starch chips (dry)
½ cup mild laundry soap (Ivory)
½ cup water

⭐ CLAY DOUGH SNOWMAN

1. Combine: ½ cup cornstarch
   1 cup baking soda
   ⅔ cup water
2. Cook in a saucepan, until very thick.
3. Cool slightly and knead one minute.
4. Form and air dry snowman.

⭐ PAPIER MACHÉ SNOWMAN

Form an actual size snowman INSIDE by crumbling newspapers and securing with masking tape.

Make 3 balls and cover with newspaper strips dipped into wall paper paste. Paint.

See: "the Snowman" by Raymond Briggs

⭐ PAPER PLATE SNOWMAN

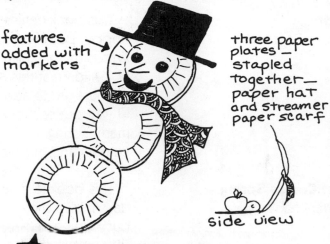

features added with markers

three paper plates — stapled together — paper hat and streamer paper scarf

side view

⭐ SOCK SNOWMAN

Stuff a sock (tube) with polyester stuffing and put elastic bands around it to make it into 4 sections. Top section is folded down to form a hat and tied off with an elastic band. Features added with marker.

⭐ STYROFOAM SNOWMAN

Use styrofoam balls connected with toothpicks. Add twigs for arms and paper cup and cardboard brim hat. Slice small section off bottom ball.

SPRING & SUMMER

Spring is here and summer's coming; what excitement! Bulbs are sprouting, eggs hatching, polliwogs swimming, birds nesting, and children bursting with energy. The following books and suggestions will help you get started.

Spring Is
Janina Domanska

This book begins, "Spring is showery, flowery, bowery....Summer is hoppy, poppy, floppy." The children will enjoy chanting the words as they watch the mischievous dachshund romp through the pages and seasons.
■ Children at this age are fascinated with language play and can be encouraged to add their own lists of rhyming words to those in the text.
■ Cut out or show pictures of signs of spring and ask children to think of as many spring words as they can. Write these words on egg, flower, or leaf cutouts and put them up on a bulletin board or a tree branch.

First Comes Spring
Anne Rockwell

This book tells about what Bear Child sees when he wakes up on a spring day. It also shows what he's wearing and what all the people in town are busy doing because it's spring. It gets warmer and Bear Child has to wear different clothing and the people in town start doing other sorts of activities because it's summer, and so it goes.
■ Discuss changes in seasons and what they mean to us. Ask questions such as, "How do we dress in springtime? Is it different in summer and the other seasons? What are some games we can play in the spring that we can't play in winter?" Plan to play one game mentioned in the play yard.
■ Plan to take a walk to look for signs of spring. Ask children to bring in signs of spring for the nature corner.

Summer Is. . .
Charlotte Zolotow

The pictures in this book are strikingly beautiful but the words by themselves make pictures, too—"Summer is porches and lemonade and dogs sleeping in the shade,...Summer is whirring lawnmowers on still afternoons and ice cream cones and watermelons." The four seasons are presented here, each with its own color palette.
■ After reading the book together, discuss the sights, sounds, and colors of each season. Talk about some of the special things that children like to do in the summer—go to the beach, picnic, have vacations, and so on.
■ Talk about the colors of summer. Read "Yellow," "Orange," "Red," and "Green" from Mary O'Neill's book of poems *Hailstones and Halibut Bones.* Ask children to wear a summer color to school the following day. (Keep a supply of ribbons to tie on those children who weren't able to wear summer colors.) Reread the color poems and talk about them.

CHANGES

YOU'LL NEED:

 colored construction paper

40" long paper

 sunflower seeds

 crayons

markers

 glue

scissors

real sunflower seeds

real sunflower seed

WHAT TO DO:

1. Cut a 40" long piece of paper and fold into five equal parts. Child glue seed to lowest panel, adds a ground line, some raindrops and yellow sunshine. Draw roots starting to grow and stem. Stem ends in top panel with flower.

2. A caterpillar shape is cut out of 8"x12" construction paper. Two more 8"x12" pieces are folded (top to bottom) and drawn to resemble butterfly wings. They are glued to both sides of caterpillar.

3. Cut an 8" long egg shape from construction paper. Cut a 12"x4" strip of paper and fold into four sections—each 3"x4". Child draws a crack on top panel and a chick in next three panels. Glue folded strip to egg. Pull out.

THE SEASONS

Since the seasons do not begin and end abruptly but really just blend in to one another and because often books are written about all four seasons, it seems appropriate to treat them together here. You may decide at times, however, that you want to concentrate on just one season. You might want to introduce any or all of the following books during circletime. Then, you can place them in the library corner so that boys and girls can explore the books independently.

Now That Days Are Colder
Aileen Fisher

There are wonderful pictures of birds, frogs, chipmunks, fish, and other animals in this book. Each animal has its own story poem.

Snow
Kathleen Todd

This book has excellent pictures of a father, a boy, and a frisky dog romping in the snow. There is very little text but children will appreciate the flavor of phrases such as, "silent footsteps follow my crunching feet."

A Year of Birds
Ashley Wolff

The brilliantly colored birds in this book should fascinate children and the information will help you explain changes in nature throughout the seasons. In the background, another change is taking place. The observant child will discover the change in Mother's shape too as the year progresses.

It's Easy to Have a Caterpillar Visit You
Caroline O'Hagan

Spring and caterpillars go together and this book tells you how to make a home for a caterpillar if you catch one and also how to feed it. Also included are some other things in nature to watch for.

Seasons
Brian Wildsmith

These bright and beautiful pictures of animals in the four seasons speak for themselves. A book like this helps children make connections from one season to the next. Be sure you allow lots of time for children to just look at these appealing pictures!

MOTIVATORS

Giving children something specific to look for in books is an excellent way to send them scurrying to the library corner. Here are some general "motivators" that will fit the books above and any other seasonal books you have.

1. Find a book that shows how differently the leaves look in the fall from the way they look in the spring.
2. Find a book that shows children and people raking or playing in the leaves.
3. Look for a book that shows animals getting ready for winter.
4. Find a book about birds and their nests.
5. Show me a book that has beach pictures in it.
6. Which book shows children playing in snow?
7. Decide which is your favorite season and bring up a book that shows what you like best. We'll read it together.

LITTLE PRINTERS

Copyright © 1987, First Teacher, Inc.

YOU'LL NEED:

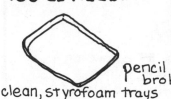

clean, styrofoam trays

pencil with broken point

brayer and water-soluable printer's ink

OR

brush and tempera paint

paper (fits inside trays)

stapler

WHAT TO DO:

1. Each child uses the broken pencil point to impress and draw a symbol of "Spring" onto the inside of the styrofoam tray. Drawings need only to be outlines—not filled in.

2. Child uses the brayer (or the brush) to spread ink (or paint) over pressed in design. Child then presses a sheet of paper into the tray and smooths it with his hand. Paper is then peeled up and allowed to dry.

3. Child makes enough of his designs so that each child in the class gets one. All the children make enough of their own designs for each classmate. Now "Spring" books are created by stapling all these different, "printed" pages together!

43

PILLOWS

YOU'LL NEED:

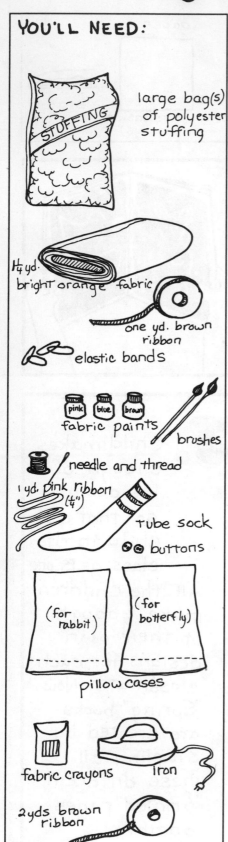

large bag(s) of polyester stuffing

H/4 yd. bright orange fabric

one yd. brown ribbon

elastic bands

fabric paints

brushes

needle and thread

1 yd. pink ribbon (1/4")

tube sock

buttons

(for rabbit) (for butterfly) pillow cases

fabric crayons   Iron

2 yds brown ribbon

WHAT TO DO:

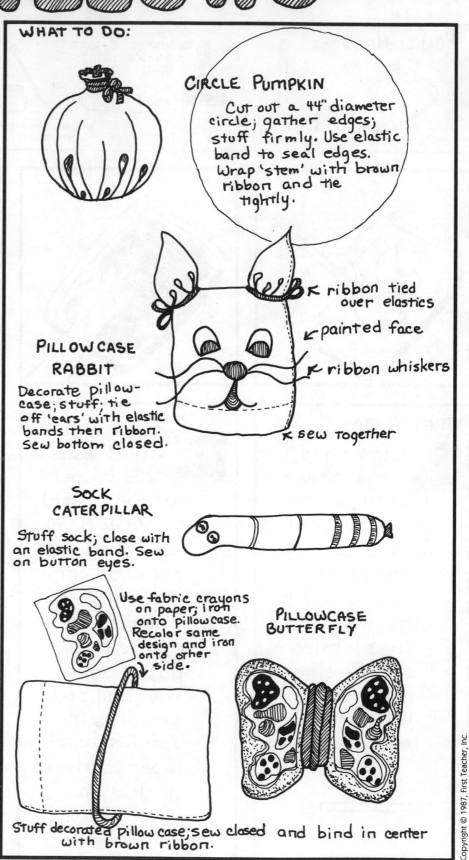

CIRCLE PUMPKIN

Cut out a 44" diameter circle; gather edges; stuff firmly. Use elastic band to seal edges. Wrap 'stem' with brown ribbon and tie tightly.

→ ribbon tied over elastics

→ painted face

→ ribbon whiskers

PILLOWCASE RABBIT

Decorate pillow-case; stuff; tie off 'ears' with elastic bands then ribbon. Sew bottom closed.

← sew together

SOCK CATERPILLAR

Stuff sock; close with an elastic band. Sew on button eyes.

Use fabric crayons on paper; iron onto pillowcase. Recolor same design and iron onto other side.

PILLOWCASE BUTTERFLY

Stuff decorated pillow case; sew closed and bind in center with brown ribbon.

44

BIBLIOGRAPHY

Adelson, Leone. *All Ready for Winter*. David McKay, 1952. (Winter)

Agee, Jon. *If Snow Falls*. Pantheon, 1982. (Winter)

Bancroft, Henrietta and Richard G. Van Gelder. *Animals in Winter*. Thomas Y. Crowell, 1963. (Winter)

Barklem, Jill. *Autumn Story*. Philomel, 1980. (Fall)

_____ . *Spring Story*. Philomel, 1980. (Spring)

_____ . *Summer Story*. Philomel, 1980. (Summer)

_____ . *Winter Story*. Philomel, 1980. (Winter)

Berenstain, Stan and Jan. *The Bears' Vacation*. Random House, 1968. (Summer)

Boon, Emilie. *It's Spring, Peterkin*. Random House, 1986. (Spring)

Branley, Franklyn. *Sunshine Makes the Seasons*. Thomas Y. Crowell, 1985. (Seasons)

Briggs, Raymond. *The Snowman*. Random House, 1978. (Winter)

Buckley, Helen. *Josie and the Snow*. Lothrop, Lee & Shepherd, 1967. (Winter)

Buscaglia, Leo. *The Fall of Freddie the Leaf*. Holt, Rinehart & Winston, 1982. (Fall)

Cartwright, Sally. *Sunlight*. Coward, McCann & Geoghegan, 1978. (Spring)

Craft, Ruth. *The Winter Bear*. Atheneum, 1975. (Winter)

Crews, Donald. *Parade*. Greenwillow, 1983. (Summer)

Cuyler, Margery. *The All-Around Pumpkin Book*. Holt, Rinehart & Winston, 1980. (Fall)

_____ . *Mouse Days: A Book of Seasons*. Holt, Rinehart & Winston, 1980. (Seasons.)

Domanska, Janina. *Spring Is*. Greenwillow, 1976. (Spring, Seasons)

Fisher, Aileen. *I Like Weather*. Thomas Y. Crowell, 1963. (Fall, Seasons)

_____ . *Now That Days Are Colder*. Bowmar, 1973. (Winter)

Garelick, May. *Down to the Beach*. Four Winds, 1973. (Summer)

Gundersheimer, Karen. *Happy Winter*. Harper & Row, 1982. (Winter)

Hader, Berta and Elmer. *The Big Snow*. Macmillan, 1948. (Winter)

Hopkins, Lee Bennett, comp. *Moments*. Harcourt, Brace & Jovanovich, 1980. (Seasons)

_____ . *The Sky Is Full of Song*. Harper & Row, 1983. (Seasons)

Ishikawa, Satomi. *Sun Through Small Leaves*. Collins-World, 1980. (Spring)

Keats, Ezra Jack. *The Snowy Day*. Viking, 1962. (Winter)

Kuskin, Karla. *In the Flaky Frosty Morning*. Harper & Row, 1969. (Winter)

Lionni, Leo. *Frederick*. Pantheon, 1967. (Fall)

Livingston, Myra Cohn. *A Circle of Seasons*. Holiday House, 1982. (Seasons)

McCloskey, Robert. *Time of Wonder*. Viking, 1957. (Summer)

McLaughlin, Lisa. *Why Won't Winter Go?* Lothrop, Lee & Shepherd, 1983. (Winter)

Oechsli, Helen and Kelly. *In My Garden*. Macmillan, 1985. (Spring, Summer).

O'Hagan, Caroline. *It's Easy to Have a Caterpillar Visit You*. Lothrop, Lee & Shepard, 1980. (Spring)

Ormondroyd, Edward. *Johnny Castleseed*. Parnassus, 1985. (Summer)

Paterson, Diane. *The Biggest Snowstorm Ever*. Dial, 1978. (Winter)

Provensen, Alice and Martin. *A Book of Seasons*. Random House, 1976. (Seasons)

_____. *The Year at Maple Hill Farm*. Atheneum, 1978. (Seasons)

Rockwell, Anne. *First Comes Spring*. Thomas Y. Crowell, 1985. (Spring)

Selsam, Millicent and Joyce Hunt. *A First Look at Leaves*. Walker, 1972. (Spring)

_____. *A First Look at the World of Plants*. Walker, 1978. (Spring)

Todd, Kathleen. *Snow*. Addison-Wesley, 1982. (Winter)

Tufari, Nancy. *All Year Long*. Greenwillow, 1983. (Seasons)

Turkle, Brinton. *Over the River and Through the Woods*. (Fall)

Vasiliu, Marcea. *A Day at the Beach*. Random House, 1977. (Summer)

Wheeler, Cindy. *Marmalade's Nap*. Random House, 1983. (Spring)

_____. *Marmalade's Snowy Day*. Random House, 1982. (Winter)

_____. *Marmalade's Yellow Leaf*. Random House, 1982. (Fall)

_____. *Rose*. Random House, 1985. (Summer)

Wildsmith, Brian. *Seasons*. Oxford, 1980. (Seasons)

Wise, William. *All on a Summer Day*. Pantheon, 1971. (Summer)

Wolff, Ashley. *A Year of Birds*. Dodd, Mead, 1984. (Seasons)

Yektai, Niki. *Sun Rain*. Four Winds, 1984. (Spring, Summer)

Zolotow, Charlotte. *Summer Is....* Abelard Schuman, 1967. (Summer, Seasons)

WORDS

WORDS

Most children at this wonderful stage of language development seem to be constantly chattering and asking questions. Enjoy using the books and ideas listed below as stepping stones to word play and other activities.

A Hole is to Dig
Ruth Krauss

This small, square-format book is a classic. Filled with deft definitions and Sendak's dancing drawings, this book brings chuckles and is great for just plain reading and rereading.

■ Read the book with children discussing those definitions that seem to have special appeal. Talk about the definition of mashed potatoes and see if children can create definitions for their favorite foods. If they need help, talk about different words to describe foods, such as: *tart, sweet, crunchy, crispy, crumbly*. Then, give them a pattern to follow: "Lemons are to pucker your mouth. Carrots are to _____ . Bananas are to _____ ."

■ Use the picture in this book or bring in a picture of a dog kissing someone. Discuss other animals or pets and their ways of displaying affection. Using "Dogs are to kiss people" as an example, let children add definitions to the following: 1) Cats are to _____ . ; 2) Teddy bears are to _____ . ; 3) Robins are to _____ .

More Than One
Tana Hoban

This striking book of photographs introduces the collective nouns *row, stack, bundle, pile, and herd*. However, there is more than one way to look at each page and each way is correct. Each child will be able to identify the obvious concept illustrated in the foreground with one word in boldface type underneath it. Some of the children will be able to look at the picture more closely and identify other objects in the background.

■ The pictures alone are meant to be lingered over. This is an exciting book for the child who likes puzzles—an excellent book to introduce and then leave out for further reading by individual children.

■ After this book has been read and reread, discuss other things that form groups and for which we have special names. Talk about one child—a group of children; one block—a stack of blocks; a single flower—a bunch of flowers; one egg—a dozen eggs. See what children can add.

Sound Words
Joan Hanson

This book will painlessly introduce words that sound like what they mean. These words that imitate natural sounds are sometimes called "echoic words." Children will respond to the pictures of the blue, bloblike faces which illustrate the meanings of words like *jingle, rattle, thud, fizz, and swat*.

■ Read the book, showing the pictures and letting children play with the words by chanting them. Ask one child to repeat one word three times (*fizz, fizz, fizz*) while another is saying a different word (*clonk*) four times. Experiment with different words and patterns.

■ Talk about things that jingle, fizz, pop, or rattle. Ask a child to think of a word that sounds like what it is and pantomime it, such as *crunch* while pretending to eat potato chips. Other children can try to guess what the word is.

STORY CANS

WHO?
- Peter Rabbit
- The Gingerbread Man
- a witch
- a super hero

WHAT?
- found a treasure
- had a dream
- found a key
- ran away

WHEN?
- at midnight
- in the rain
- at the wrong time
- just in time

WHERE?
- in a castle
- in a boat
- at the store
- in outer space

YOU'LL NEED:

4 one-pound coffee cans with plastic lids

sticky labels

craft knife (adult use only)

markers

1" x 5" strips of paper

WHAT TO DO:

1. Adult cuts a star shape in each plastic lid; it should be large enough for a child's fist to fit through.

2. Adult and children think up characters, places, times and situations together. Each is written on a strip of paper. (Pictures can be used, also)

3. Place the character strips in the can labeled "Who"; the places in "Where"; the times in "When" and the situations into "What". Use question marks.

4. Line up the cans in the following order: "WHO", "WHAT", "WHEN", "WHERE"

5. Children pick one strip from each can. Teacher reads it aloud (or child identifies the pictures)

6. Child uses his selections to make up a simple story - to tell, to illustrate or make a book.

WORDS

If you look over your book corner for books about words, you may find that you'll need to borrow some from the library to supplement your collection. You might want to introduce any or all of the following books during a time when the group is together. Then, place the books in the library corner so that children can explore and discuss them on their own.

When
Leo Lionni

This book is all about what *when* means. Questions such as, "When will I see a rainbow? When will puppies open their eyes?" are asked and illustrated. Children will have fun guessing what the questions are and they may even know the answers.

Sky Dragon
Ron Wegen

Did you ever watch clouds in the sky and think that some of them looked like animals? This book will turn on everybody's imagination as they examine the pictures carefully to find new and wonderful hidden things.

A Scale Full of Fish
Naomi Bossom

On one page of this book is a scale full of fish and on the facing page is a fish full of scales. The words on each page are just turned around, with illustrations for each saying.

Is It Rough? Is It Smooth?
Is it Shiny?
Tana Hoban

These are wonderful color photos but there aren't any words; so children will have fun supplying descriptive adjectives as they discuss each picture. You may want to ask a few questions to get them started, such as, "How does a broken bubble gum bubble feel?"

I Packed My Trunk
Barbara Walker

Some of the children may have played the game "I'm going on a trip and I'm taking _____." This book has a similar game that starts with, "I packed my trunk to go to Squintum's and in it I put/an Apple, big and red,/a Book to take to bed,/a Cookie in a sack,/a Duck who says _____." Children will enjoy looking at the pictures and guessing the rhymes.

Opposites
John Burningham

Direct attention to a specific page by saying, "Look at this page! Here he's nice and dry, but on the next page, he's just the opposite. He's _____."

Listening for Sounds
Adelaide Holl

This book is all about things that make sounds. Children learn that there are all kinds of sounds—quiet sounds, animal sounds, building sounds, soft sounds, and so on. Each page shows different sound makers.

MOTIVATORS

Use some of these "stimulators" to encourage children to explore the books and to discover new and unusual meanings of words.

1. Find a book that shows objects which make sounds.
2. What book shows pictures of items that look the same?
3. Find a book that will help you discover how objects feel.
4. Which book uses words that make you laugh?
5. Find the book that shows your favorite kind of words and bring it to me so we can read it together.

WORD TREE

YOU'LL NEED:

large sheet of brown paper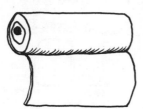

colored construction paper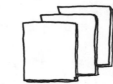

markers

Read Shel Silverstein's "THE GIVING TREE"

(leaves reading: friendly, shares, smile, laughs, funny, kind, cute, nice, neat, helpful, happy)

1. WHAT TO DO:

Read the story, cut out and pin up a paper tree. Discuss all the nice things you can say about others. Adult can encourage children to think about their classmates and say 'good' things about each other.

2.

Cut out leaf shapes from construction paper, write (or draw) a descriptive word on each leaf. Children tape up each leaf. Add a leaf when someone 'sees' or 'does' something nice.

3. Variations:

Place a photo of one child in the center of the Giving Tree. Everyone uses 'good' words to refer to that particular child, or put up 'good' deeds.

texture book

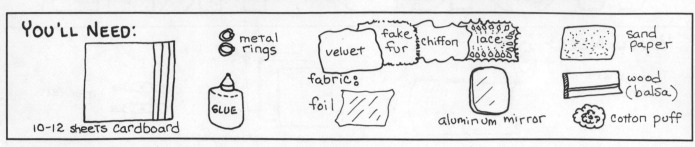

YOU'LL NEED:

10-12 sheets cardboard

GLUE

metal rings

fabric:
veluet fake fur chiffon lace
foil

aluminum mirror

sand paper

wood (balsa)

cotton puff

WHAT TO DO:

1. Collect and cut out as many of above suggested materials as possible. Discuss textures and use words such as rough, smooth, puffy, and so on.

2. Glue each piece to both sides of cardboard sheets, making sure there is a contrast in texture on each 'page'.

3. Punch two holes into left side of each cardboard 'page'. Insert metal rings. Use book for discussion, to play 'match', to enhance vocabulary.

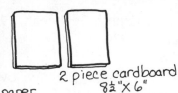

BOOK BINDING

MY PHOTOS by Juan   **KIM'S BOOK**

YOU'LL NEED:

8 sheets 8½"x11" paper

2 piece cardboard 8½"X6"

 carpet/button thread and large-eye needle

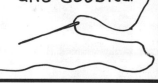 colorful plastic tape (mending tape found in grocery and discount stores)

 white glue

WHAT TO DO:

1. Adult folds eight pages in half to make 16 pages. Each page will measure 8½"X5½".

2. Poke three holes along center fold. Holes should go through all pages.

3. Thread button thread onto needle, but do not make a knot. It should be long and doubled.

1. sew down through center hole.
2. sew up through top hole.
3. sew over to and down through bottom hole.
4. sew up through center hole again.
5. Tie a knot with two ends. (around thread from hole 1 to 3)

4. Decorate two cardboard covers. Glue these covers to first and last pages of book so spine of book sticks out of cardboard covers ¼".

cover
↑spine (¼" left exposed)

5. Cut a piece of tape 1" taller than book.

6. Place tape so half of it is on front cover along spine. Fold other half backwards smoothly over spine to back cover.

7. Open book and pull pages forward at the top and bottom while you tuck tape over top of covers and to inside of book. Repeat with bottom piece of tape.

BIBLIOGRAPHY

Bossom, Naomi. *A Scale Full of Fish*. Greenwillow, 1979.

Burningham, John. *Opposites*. Crown, 1985.

Gag, Wanda. *Millions of Cats*. Coward, McCann & Geohegan, 1928.

Hanson, Joan. *More Sound Words*. Lerner, 1979.

_____ . *Sound Words*. Lerner, 1976.

Hoban, Tana. *Is It Rough? Is It Smooth? Is It Shiny?*. Greenwillow, 1984.

_____ . *More Than One*. Greenwillow, 1981.

Holl, Adelaide. *Listening for Sounds*. Golden Press, n.d.

Krauss, Ruth. *A Hole Is to Dig*. Harper & Row, 1982.

Kuskin, Karla. *Near the Window Tree*. Harper & Row, 1975.

Lionni, Leo. *What?*. Pantheon, 1983.

_____ . *When?*. Pantheon, 1983.

_____ . *Where?*. Pantheon, 1983.

_____ . *Who?*. Pantheon, 1983.

_____ . *Words to Talk About*. Pantheon, 1985.

Moncure, Jane Belk. *Happy Birthday Word Bird*. Child's Word, 1983.

Morley, Diana. *Marms in the Marmalade*. Carolrhoda Books, 1986.

Piper, Watty. *The Little Engine That Could*. Platt, Munk, 1930.

Schwartz, Alvin. *A Twister of Twists, A Tangler of Tongues*. Lippincott, 1972.

Seuss, Dr. *The Cat in the Hat*. Random House, 1957.

Shecter, Ben. *Sparrow Song*. Harper & Row, 1981.

Walker, Barbara. *I Packed My Trunk*. Follett, 1969.

Wegen, Ron. *Sky Dragon*. Greenwillow, 1982.

Wood, Audrey. *Quick as a Cricket*. Child's Play, 1982.

COLORS

COLORS

One of the best ways to expand children's understanding of colors is to present them with books in which colors play a big part, including heavily illustrated ones and those in which "colors" are the major theme.

Is It Red? Is It Yellow?
Is It Blue?
Tana Hoban

· This book's four-color photographs present real-life examples that lend themselves to discussions of colors. Below each photo, dots of the colors in that illustration are shown.

■ Read the story. Pass out circles of red, yellow, blue, orange, green, and purple construction paper so that each child has one. Show each picture in turn, but cover the dots. Ask children with the matching colors to show their circles.

■ Have the construction paper circles mentioned above nearby. Pick out objects in the room or clothing children are wearing with one or more of the six colors discussed. Indicate the item and have children show its colors by holding up the matching circles.

Green Says Go
Ed Emberley

First, the three primary colors—red, blue, yellow—and then black and white are shown; next, the mixing of primary colors and an explanation of shades can be seen. At the end, the colors "talk."

■ Discuss different colors that children see in or on their way to school. If necessary, remind them of objects and events such as the following: stop signs, traffic lights with their changing colors, school buses, fire engines, leaves, school crossing guards' belts or vests, and so on.

■ Talk about the ways that colors might "talk" to people. Begin with the objects mentioned above. Then, ask some of the questions given in the book such as, "What color says hot? Cold? Summer?"

The Mixed-Up Chameleon
Eric Carle

A bored chameleon that wants to look like other animals lands on them to try to satisfy its wish. The lizard ends up still unhappy.

■ After reading the story, discuss the colors of the animals on which the chameleon landed. Have different colors of construction paper or colored clay chameleons nearby. Give each child a chance to choose a color or chameleon and to name an animal that is the same color. (If you have any types of three-dimensional animals in the room, display them as props.)

■ Play the CHAMELEON GAME on page 57.

Spring Green
Valerie M. Selkowe

At Woody Woodchuck's spring party, a prize will be given for the best "green" thing. Donny Duck can't think of anything to take, but comes with an unusual solution in the last pages of the story.

■ Before you finish reading the story, stop and ask children, "If you were going to Woody's party, what would you bring?" Allow time for each child to make a suggestion about a "green" thing.

■ Ask children to think of different types of celebrations. Have them decide on a "special" color for each event and to explain why they choose that particular color. Then, let them decide what they might bring.

THE CHAMELEON GAME

YOU'LL NEED:

colored construction paper

scissors

PATTERN

WHAT TO DO:

 1. Adult or child cuts chameleon shapes from colored papers, using pattern above. Give these chameleons to one half of a group of children to hide. Others leave room.

 2. Children hide chameleons, in plain sight, on an object that matches the chameleon's color. The chameleon will blend with background.

 3. The other half of the group of children come back into the room and search for chameleons. Children with the most chameleons win this game.

COLORS

Many of the books in your library corner will be heavily illustrated. You may wish, however, to go to the library to find books whose themes are color. Make a book display and let children have a chance to see all the different shades. You might want to introduce any or all of the following books before children do any exploring on their own.

Brown Is Beautiful
Jean Bond

This books concentrates on showing earthy colored objects found in three places that children may be familiar with—farm, city, beach.

Colors
John Reiss

Colors are introduced one at a time. Many examples of objects showing each color are given.

Freight Train
Donald Crews

The author/illustrator uses seven distinctive cars of a freight train to show off an equal number of different colors.

Tomato and Other Colors
Ivan Chermayeff

Here the theme is that color can serve many purposes and that each sends along different "messages." Children have a chance to "read" these messages as they look at similar ideas presented in various media.

What Is Pink?
Christina Rossetti

This depiction of a verse written long ago shows what happens when some type of white or black dye is added to familiar colors. Children will have a chance to look at light and dark shades of different colors.

What Is the Color of the Wide, Wide World
Margaret Friskey

Each animal or insect thinks that the world is a different color because each lives in a different colored environment.

Mr. Rabbit and the Lovely Present
Charlotte Zolotow

A rabbit wants the right "colorful" present for her mother so choices are mentioned for each color and the best one is chosen. The rabbit has interesting reasons for deciding which suggestions won't work out.

I Like Red
Marie Norkin Warach

In this book, children see at least five or six examples of objects that often appear in certain colors. Good for introducing or reviewing color names.

MOTIVATORS

Try some of these motivators to send children into further book explorations. They will fit one or more of the books above and any other books that you have collected as "colorful" books.
1. Find a book that is about just one color.
2. What book would give you ideas if you were going on a "red" color treasure hunt?
3. What book might help you decide on the colors to make sky, grass, or a tree in a picture?
4. Find a book that shows you colors that are light shades or dark shades.
5. Find a book that shows your favorite color. Let's read it together.

WHO DREW THE PICTURES?

YOU'LL NEED:

long sheet of paper from a roll

books

crayons
markers
paints
brushes
scissors

OUR FAVORITE ANIMALS

by LIZA, HOWIE, TOYA

Then a rainbow appeared in the sky over the city.

WHAT TO DO:

1. Adult reads several books to children that have been illustrated by the same person. Point out and discuss the style and media used.

2. Include a discussion of Ezra Jack Keats' use of painted or drawn backgrounds with collaged cut-outs. Brian Wildsmith uses colorful designs and Eric Carle uses paints with cut-outs.

3. Have children experiment with these media and in the style of the particular illustrator.
☆ Illustrations should NOT be a copy of the illustrator's material — just the 'feel' of it!

4. Help children design 3 or 4 large poster-sized illustrations using the style and media of a particular illustrator on each one.

5. Adult labels each poster with a title or sentence so that each looks like the cover on or a page in a book.

6. Adult can hang these on the doors in the book corner. Now, you have GIANT books and pages with lots of color to brighten up the book corner.

COLOR PICNIC

YOU'LL NEED:

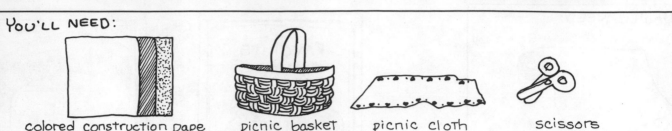

colored construction pape | picnic basket | picnic cloth | scissors

bread?
brownie?
chocolate cake?

tomato?
apple?
pizza?

lettuce?
cabbage?
melon?

WHAT TO DO:

1. Adult and children cut out many colored shapes of all sizes. Pile shapes into a picnic basket with a cloth.

2. Children "go on a picnic" and use these shapes to decide what foods they've taken along.

3. Child pulls out a shape, using color as a clue, and names a food that comes in or is made in that shape. Make funny foods, too!

COLOR MAZE

a.   b.   c.   d.   e.   f.

YOU'LL NEED:

(approx. 11" x 9")
one sheet cardboard

(10¾" x 8¼")
4 sheets of clear acetate

red
blue
green
markers

plain paper

masking Tape

WHAT TO DO:

1. Adult uses masking tape to attach acetate sheet to cardboard along top edge. Repeat until you have three acetate sheets attached to cardboard at the top. (See step "a." above.)

2. Now attach the last acetate sheet, with masking tape, to the <u>bottom</u> of the cardboard, opposite the top tape.

(See step "b." above)

3. Insert, directly on the cardboard, a sheet of paper on which you've drawn a doghouse in the lower right-hand corner and a dog in the upper left-hand corner. ("c.")

4. Now flip one sheet of acetate down and draw, in a <u>red</u> pen, a scribble line from the dog to the doghouse. (See step "d." above)

5. Flip down the second acetate sheet and draw, in <u>blue</u> pen, a scribble line from the dog to the doghouse. Repeat procedure with next sheet of acetate and <u>green</u> pen. ("e.")

6. The child now uses a marker to trace a 'route' from dog to doghouse OVER ONE COLOR SCRIBBLE ONLY! — on the last acetate sheet overlay. Child checks route by flipping to that one color page and matching

BIBLIOGRAPHY

Bond, Jean. *Brown is Beautiful*. Franklin Watts, 1969.

Bright, Robert. *I Like Red*. Doubleday, 1955.

Brunhoff, Laurent de. *Babar's Book of Color*. Random House, 1984.

Burningham, John. *John Burningham's Colors*. Crown, 1985.

Carle, Eric. *The Mixed-Up Chameleon*. Thomas Y. Crowell, 1984.

Chermayeff, Ivan. *Tomato and Other Colors*. Prentice Hall, 1980.

Crews, Donald. *Freight Train*. Greenwillow, 1978.

Emberley, Ed. *Green Says Go*. Little, Brown, 1968.

Freeman, Don. *The Chalk Box Story*. Lippincott, 1976.

_____ . *A Rainbow of My Own*. Viking, 1966.

Friskey, Margaret. *What Is the Color of the Wide, Wide World?*. Children's Press, 1973.

Gomi, Taro. *Where's the Fish?* Morrow, 1986.

Gundersheimer, Karen. *Colors to Show*. Harper & Row, 1986.

Hoban, Tana. *Is It Red? Is It Yellow? Is It Blue?* Greenwillow, 1978.

Karn, George. *Circus Colors*. Little, Brown, 1986.

Koelling, Caryl. *A Surprise for Your Eyes*. Intervisual, 1981.

Lionni, Leo. *A Color of His Own*. Pantheon, 1975.

Peek, Merle. *Mary Wore Her Red Dress and Henry Wore His Green Sneakers*. Clarion, 1985.

Reiss, John. *Colors*. Bradbury, 1969.

Rossetti, Christina. *What Is Pink?* Macmillan, 1971.

Savage, Dorothy. *The Green Peephole Book*. Dutton, 1986.

Selkowe, Valerie. *Spring Green*. Lothrop, Lee & Shepard, 1985.

Spier, Peter. *Oh, Were They Ever Happy!*. Doubleday, 1978.

Testa, Fulvio. *If You Take a Paintbrush*. Dial, 1982.

Warach, Marie. *I Like Red*. Dandelion Books, 1979.

Zolotow, Charlotte. *Mr. Rabbit and the Lovely Present*. Harper & Row, 1962.

MATH

MATH

Children delight in bringing mathematics concepts into their conversations and books can help expand their knowledge about the many different areas included in this subject—number recognition, geometry (shapes), measurement (size), patterns, probability and statistics, and logic. The books below present some important math concepts.

The Circle Sarah Drew
Peter and Susan Barrett

After Sarah draws a circle, her friends decide what she could make from that shape.

■ Discuss the illustrations so that children will be introduced to circular-shaped items that appear in their daily lives—manhole covers, duck ponds, the full moon, and so on. Then, ask the questions given at the end of the book, "What do you think it is?"

■ Let each child feel a circular bead (a three-dimensional shape) or a ring (a two-dimensional shape). Ask them to look around the room and name an object that has the same shape.

Listen to a Shape
Marcia Brown

Through its photographs and simple text, this book acquaints children with how shapes "talk." They listen to descriptive words like *round, pointed, square, crescent,* and *triangle* and look at real-life examples.

■ Read the book aloud. Then, ask children to recall one of the descriptive nouns or adjectives given. Find that page again. Let various children explain what that word means to them. Write down each definition on a chart. Continue on. Later, read a definition and have children point out examples.

■ Have blocks, straws, yarn, and other manipulative materials nearby. Ask children to recall some of the words they heard as the book was read. Let them use the materials to form shapes on a feltboard or lapboard.

Is It Larger? Is It Smaller?
Tana Hoban

Through Hoban's photographs, side-by-side examples of similar objects or people are presented so children can see differences in size.

■ Ask a child in the group to choose two similar objects that will demonstrate size differences. Have the child stand the two objects up, point to one, and ask the questions from the book title. Let other children in the group answer the questions.

■ Stand two children back to back. Have children ask similar questions to those in the book title, inserting a child's name in place of the pronouns.

Count on Clifford
Norman Bridwell

This story about Clifford's birthday shows differing amounts of objects to illustrate each number symbol.

■ After the story has been read, let a child pick out a number name. Have another child find the appropriate page in the book and choose one group of objects to be counted, and then point to each item as the group counts.

■ Help children tell their own versions of Clifford's birthday. The first time an amount of objects is suggested, draw or have a child draw simple pictures of the objects on the chalkboard or a chart.

BUILD·A·BOOK

YOU'LL NEED:

7 pieces of paper

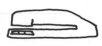 crayons

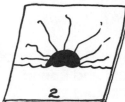 stapler

1. WHAT TO DO:
Child makes this 7 page book by making each page separately. Pages are put together, and then child makes up a story that is dictated by what has happened to each page.

2.
Trace child's hand on page one – in an unusual shape – to create the character.

3.
Child draws a time of day on page two. (morning, midnight, sunset, noon)

4.
Child tears holes into page three (or pokes holes with a pencil).

5.
Child crinkles up page 4, then reopens it.

6.
Child folds page 5 every which way, then reopens it.

7.
Child draws a favorite scene on page 6.

8.
Child colors page 7 in one solid color. Staple pages together to make a book.

9.
Child adds features to hand tracing 'character' on page 1; gives it a name and tells a story about the character as he goes from page to page. (Adult might want to write in story.)

MATH

You will need to decide whether you want to concentrate in the library corner on one area in mathematics, such as number recognition, and place just those kinds of books there or whether you want to have all types of math books available. Any library will be able to find books to fit in any of the categories. You might want to introduce any or all of the following books during group times before children have free time to explore them on their own.

Are You Square?
Ethel and Leonard Kessler

Most pages in this book show examples of different geometric shapes; at the end, children find out that certain shapes tell them and drivers what to do.

Round and Round and Round
Tana Hoban

Here children will see photographs of many objects that illustrate two- and three-dimensional circular shapes as a whole or as one of their parts.

The Elephant's Nest
Marilee Robin Burton

This wordless book about animals and their homes contains lots of number groupings that "beg" to be identified as the story is being told.

What's Happening?
Heather Amery

In this story about building a castle at the beach, children will see groups of objects such as flags and buckets being used. They can easily note and describe the number and shapes of the flags or the sizes and shapes of the buckets that were used to make the castle.

John Burningham's 1 2 3
John Burningham

As children look at the book, they will be able to count groups as ten children climb a tree. (At the end, a surprise visitor comes!)

When Sheep Can't Sleep
Satoshi Kitamura

A sheep has trouble sleeping so it decides to count different objects instead of the old-time, sleep-inducing remedy—sheep. Children can join in to try to make the sheep drowsy.

Shapes
Janet Williams

In this book, children can see what can be made with different-colored geometric shapes when one or more kinds are combined.

MOTIVATORS

Here are some suggestions you have want to use to motivate children toward examining books and discovering what new or familiar facts about mathematics they can find.
1. Find a book that shows shapes and where you can find them as you look around in the room or outside.
2. Find a book that tells how to make things out of shapes.
3. Which book shows lots of objects that look like a circle or a ball?
4. Show me a book about numbers.
5. Find a book that has pictures that show objects or people who are different sizes.
6. Find a book with a picture of your favorite shape and we'll read it.

shape bulletin board

YOU'LL NEED:

scissors

colored construction paper

 tape

 crayons

WHAT TO DO:

1. Adult and child cut out □'s, ▭'s, △'s, O's in various colors and sizes.
Children discuss how shapes can be made into vehicles and buildings.

2. Adult sets up a bulletin board for children to add these vehicles and buildings. Children can draw in details for this "City Scene"

3. Use the same shapes to create a country, underwater, outer space bulletin board.

IN THE CITY...

design·a·line book

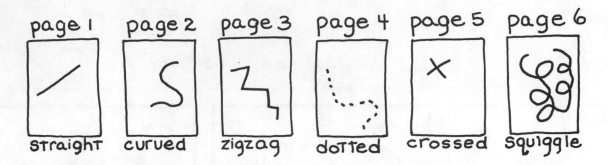

page 1 — straight
page 2 — curved
page 3 — zigzag
page 4 — dotted
page 5 — crossed
page 6 — squiggle

YOU'LL NEED:

6 pieces of paper (per book)

stapler

markers

WHAT TO DO:

1. Adult staples together six sheets of paper to form one book. Make six books. Have six children sit in a circle. Each child draws one straight line on the first page.

2. Children turn to page two and pass books to child on left. All children now draw one curved line on page two. (The line can be placed anywhere on the page.)

3. Children turn to the next page and pass the books to child on left. All children now draw one zigzag line on page 3.

4. Children continue to make one line on a page (see above suggestions) and pass the books to the left, until each child gets his/her own back.

5. Children then use the lines on each page to form pictures. They can color in the squiggle design. They can label each picture, if desired.

6. Use this activity with some of these books:
"The Circle Sarah Drew"
"The Line Sophie Drew"
"Lines, Spines and Porcupines"
"Harold and the Purple Crayon"

counting book

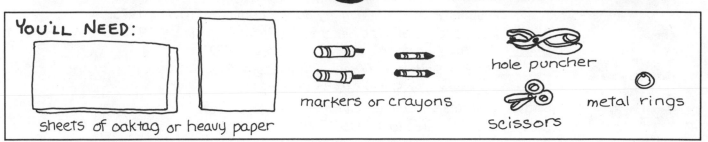

YOU'LL NEED:

sheets of oaktag or heavy paper

markers or crayons

hole puncher

scissors

metal rings

WHAT TO DO:

1. Adult assembles each part as shown here. Punch a hole in each part and put all together with a metal ring.

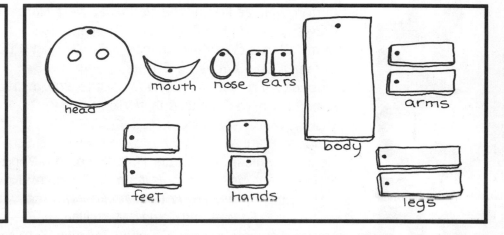

head

mouth

nose

ears

body

arms

feet

hands

legs

---

2. Each child either draws on features or makes tracings and prints on each of the shapes. Put the correct number of teeth, fingers etc. and draw in that number.

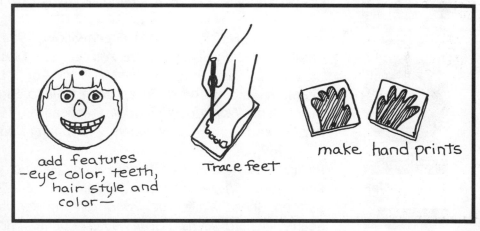

add features —eye color, teeth, hair style and color—

Trace feet

make hand prints

---

3. Start the book with the head and assemble the rest as pages behind that. Book can also be taken apart and assembled, like a puzzle, to form a figure.

Amery, Heather. *What's Happening?* Usborne, 1984.

Anno, Mitsumasa. *Anno's Counting Book.* Thomas Y. Crowell, 1975.

Barrett, Peter and Susan. *The Circle Sarah Drew.* Scroll Press, 1972.

_____ . *The Line Sophie Drew.* Scroll Press, 1972.

_____ . *The Square Ben Drew.* Scroll Press, 1972.

Brenner, Barbara. *The Snow Parade.* Crown, 1984.

Bridwell, Norman. *Count on Clifford.* Scholastic, 1985.

Brown, Marcia. *Listen to a Shape.* Franklin Watts, 1979.

Burningham, John. *John Burningham's 1 2 3.* Crown, 1985.

Burton, Marilee Robin. *The Elephant's Nest.* Harper & Row, 1979.

Crews, Donald. *Ten Black Dots.* Scribner's, 1986.

Demi. *Demi's Count the Animals 1 2 3.* Grosset & Dunlap, 1986.

Dreamer, Sue. *Circus 1 2 3.* Little, Brown, 1985.

Emberley, Ed. *The Wing of a Flea.* Little, Brown, 1961.

Fisher, Leonard Everett. *Boxes!* Viking, 1984.

Friskey, Margaret. *Chicken Little, Count-to-Ten.* Children's Press, 1946.

Galdone, Paul. *Over in the Meadow.* Simon & Schuster, 1986.

Hague, Kathleen. *NumBears.* Holt, Rinehard & Winston, 1986.

Hoban, Tana. *Is It Larger? Is It Smaller?.* Greenwillow, 1985.

_____ . *Round and Round and Round.* Greenwillow, 1983.

_____ . *Shapes and Things.* Macmillan, 1970.

Howe, Caroline Walton. *Counting Penguins Zero to Nine.* Harper & Row, 1983.

Jonas, Ann. *Holes and Peeks.* Greenwillow, 1984.

Kessler, Ethel and Leonard. *Are You Square?.* Doubleday, 1966.

_____ . *Two, Four, Six, Eight: A Book About Legs.* Dodd, Mead, 1980.

Kitamura, Satoshi. *When Sheep Cannot Sleep.* Farrar, Straus, Giroux, 1986.

Miller, Jane. *Farm Counting Book.* Prentice-Hall, 1983.

Peppe, Rodney. *Circus Numbers, A Counting Book.* Farrar, Straus, Giroux, 1969.

Phillips, Jo. *Right Angles: Paper-Folding Geometry.* Harper & Row, 1972.

Reiss, John. *Shapes.* Bradbury, 1974.

Samton, Sheila White. *The World from My Window.* Crown, 1985.

Scarry, Richard. *Richard Scarry's Best Counting Book.* Random House, 1972.

Schwartz, David. *How Much Is a Million?.* Lothrop, Lee & Shephard, 1986.

Sitomer, Mindel and Harry. *Zero Is Not Nothing.* Thomas Y. Crowell, 1978.

Tafuri, Nancy. *Who's Counting?.* Greenwillow, 1986.

Testa, Fulvio. *If You Look Around You.* Dial, 1983.

Tudor, Tasha. *1 Is One.* Walck, 1956.

Williams, Janet. *Shapes.* Ernest Benn, 1970.

Zolotow, Charlotte. *One Step, Two.* Lothrop, Lee & Shepard, 1955.

ABC

ABC

Children's early lives are full of words they hear. Then, they begin to "see" words and to learn about the ABCs. At some point, children understand the connection between the letters and the words. One way to enhance that bridge is through alphabet books. The books below can be used to introduce each letter or to talk about the special words.

A Is for Angry
Sandra Boynton

Animals are introduced using the letters of the alphabet in order and with an alliterative adjective or two.

■ Read the story the first time without giving some of the adjectives. After explaining in simple terms what alliteration means and giving examples from the book such as "big bashful bear," let children suggest some of the adjectives.

■ Pick five children whose first names start with letters in the first third of the alphabet (A-H). Write their names on a piece of chart paper and have a child underline the first letter in each one. Help children arrange themselves in ABC order according to the first letter in their names. Continue on with the rest of the group and other letters.

Ed Emberley's A B C
Ed Emberley

Animals are doing different activities to form letters; in the pictures are also objects whose names start with the letters being made.

■ After the story has been read once, have children describe in their own words how each letter has been formed. Let different ones follow the directions and try to make the letters in the sand or on a chalkboard.

■ See how many items children can identify in a picture whose names begin with the letter on that page.

AlphaBears
Kathleen Hague

A story about twenty-six teddy bears is told in rhyme; their names go in alphabetical order as the various bears appear.

■ Help children come up with alliterative names for themselves by asking them to pick one of their own names and then give themselves another one that begins with the same letter. Explain that they may make up a name or borrow one from a friend. Write the "new" name on chart paper and have children circle the matching initial letters.

■ Let children role play the different teddy bears.

Anno's Alphabet
Mitsumasa Anno

Each letter is shown carved in wood and on the facing page is shown one object whose name begins with that letter. In the border, children will see certain plants, insects, birds, and other items that also start the same way. They may discover even more listed in the back of the book.

■ Write each letter of the alphabet in the center of a piece of paper. Let children describe how they think you made the letter. Then, have them "act out" different letters.

■ Have children pick out one of the letters used above and name the letter. Ask them to suggest different objects that might be used as a full-page illustration to go with the letter.

PUFFY LETTERS

YOU'LL NEED:

 one cup flour

 one cup water

 red yellow green
 food colors

 Cotton ball

bag of cotton balls (cosmetic puffs)

WHAT TO DO:

1. Combine flour and water and stir until mixture is smooth. Pour mixture into three small bowls.

2. Add food coloring to each bowl. One bowl should be red, one bowl yellow, one bowl green. Mix contents of each bowl well.

3. Dip a cotton ball into one bowl and turn until entire ball is covered. Do not squeeze balls.

4. Place many dipped balls on lightly greased baking sheet to form a letter. Make sure each ball touches one next to it.

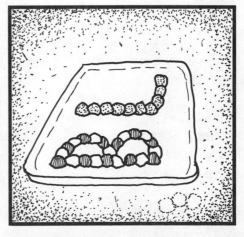

5. Bake in a 300°F oven for one hour or until lightly browned and hard. Let cool on baking sheet.

6. Mount letters on wooden plaques with glue or decorate boxes or use for children to touch and learn letters.

ABC

A current listing of available ABC books contains over one hundred fifty suggestions so it will be fun collecting a wide variety for your library corner. Try the library and bookstores. Suggest that children bring in some from their own bookshelves. You might want to introduce parts of some of the following books during circletime before putting them in the library corner.

C Is for Circus
Bernice Chardiet

In the text for each illustration in this book about circus life, at least two or three words begin with the letter being presented. Children will enjoy a "big brass band" or an "extremely elegant elephant."

John Burningham's A B C
John Burningham

This author/illustrator has chosen mostly animals—and a few other objects when mammals wouldn't fit—to present labeled items in alphabetical order.

All in the Woodland Early
Jane Yolen

In song, story, and alphabetical order, children will discover familiar and unusual forest animals that will be fun to discuss.

Animal Alphabet
Bert Kitchen

Very realistically drawn animals are doing something with the letter that begins each one's name or are perched on it. Readers are invited to name each animal. (The names are given in the back of the book.) Each page also shows other objects whose names start with the letter shown.

Farm Alphabet Book
Jane Miller

Using photographs, the author presents in alphabetical order farm animals and other farm items; more information about each is given in a sentence. Children will have fun guessing what might appear in this book.

Richard Scarry's A B C Word Book
Richard Scarry

There is a brief story for each letter of the alphabet; the letter being discussed is shown in red on that page.

On Market Street
Arnold Lobel

Through verses and illustrations, children learn about stores and shopping as they name appropriate items in alphabetical order.

MOTIVATORS

Try some of the suggested motivators that follow to stimulate children's interest in looking at the different types of alphabet books.

1. Find a book with one letter on each page and only one thing whose name begins with that letter.

2. Find a book that shows the order in which the letters in the alphabet go by showing pictures of animals and the words that say their names.

3. Find a book with the first letter of your name on a page.

4. Find a book that helps you see how the letters are made.

5. Bring me your favorite ABC book, choose a favorite letter, and tell us words that begin with that letter.

GIANT LETTERS

YOU'LL NEED:

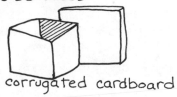
corrugated cardboard

craft knife

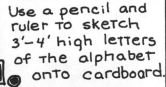
pencil
ruler

masking tape
or

latex paint

clear contact paper

WHAT TO DO:

1. Use a pencil and ruler to sketch 3'-4' high letters of the alphabet onto cardboard.

Adult uses craft knife and cuts out each letter.

2. Letter can be left as it is, or for longer wear, adult can wrap edges with masking tape or clear contact paper.

3. Children might enjoy painting each letter with latex paint or use letter to make collages with pictures.

★ have a parade ★ match a sound ★ spell a name ★ make a letter

ABC GROCERY STORE

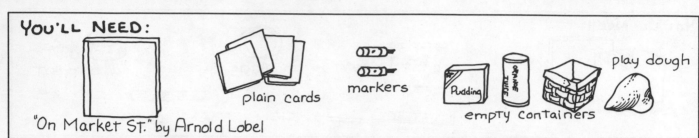

YOU'LL NEED:

"On Market St." by Arnold Lobel

plain cards

markers

empty containers — Pudding, ORANGE JUICE, play dough

WHAT TO DO:

1. Read "On Market St." by Arnold Lobel. After reading the story, set up an ABC Grocery Store in your classroom. (This is great after a trip to the market.)

2. You will need to put a card with each letter of the alphabet (combine X, Y, Z) on a different shelf or table or chair.

3. Children sort empty boxes, cans, plastic and play dough foods onto a shelf according to their first letter and sound. Add play money, cash register and bags.

WHAT'S INSIDE?

YOU'LL NEED:

a large sheet of posterboard

glue

markers

scissors

WHAT TO DO:

1. Copy this design and make a box for each letter in the alphabet. Label each box with one letter.

2. Each child picks one box and hunts for an object in the classroom (or draws the object). The object must begin with the letter on the outside of the box. Child keeps the contents of box secret.

3. Other children guess what is in the box. Sometimes clues must be given.

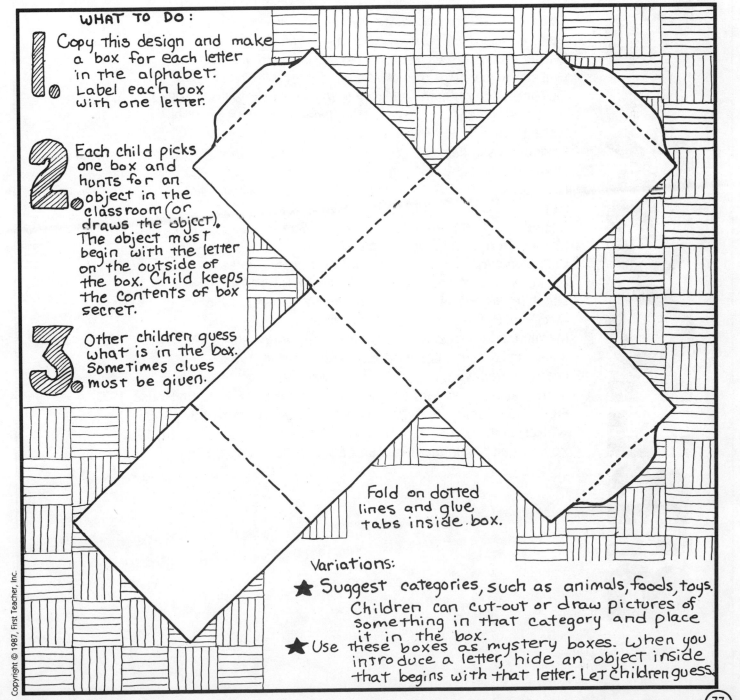

Fold on dotted lines and glue tabs inside box.

Variations:

★ Suggest categories, such as animals, foods, toys. Children can cut-out or draw pictures of something in that category and place it in the box.

★ Use these boxes as mystery boxes. When you introduce a letter, hide an object inside that begins with that letter. Let children guess.

BIBLIOGRAPHY

Anno, Mitsumasa. *Anno's Alphabet*. Thomas Y. Crowell, 1975.

Atlas, Ron. *Looking for Zebra*. Simon & Schuster, 1986.

Boynton, Sandra. *A Is for Angry*. Workman, 1983.

Brown, Marcia. *All Butterflies: An ABC Book*. Scribner's, 1974.

Burningham, John. *John Burningham's A B C*. Crown, 1985.

Chardiet, Bernice. *C Is for Circus*. Walker, 1971.

Clifton, Lucille. *The Black A B C's*. Dutton, 1970.

Crews, Donald. *We Read: A to Z*. Harper & Row, 1967.

Demi. *Demi's Find the Animal A B C*. Grosset & Dunlap, 1985.

Emberley, Ed. *Ed Emberley's A B C*. Little, Brown, 1978.

Gag, Wanda. *ABC Bunny*. Doubleday, 1965.

Gardner, Beau. *Have You Ever Seen. . .?*. Dodd, Mead, 1986.

Geisert, Arthur. *Pigs from A to Z*. Houghton Mifflin, 1986.

Gundersheimer, Karen. *ABC Say with Me*. Harper & Row, 1984.

Hague, Kathleen. *AlphaBears*. Holt, Rinehart & Winston, 1984.

Hoban, Tana. *A B See!*. Greenwillow, 1982.

Hoguet, Susan Ramsay. *I Unpacked My Grandmother's Trunk*. Dutton, 1983.

Hyman, Trina Schart. *A Little Alphabet*. Little, Brown, 1980.

Isodora, Rachel. *City Seen from A to Z*. Greenwillow, 1983.

Johnson, Crockett. *Harold's ABC*. Harper & Row, 1963.

Kitamura, Satoshi. *What's Inside*. Farrar, Straus & Giroux, 1985.

Kitchen, Bert. *Animal Alpabet*. Dial, 1984.

Lillie, Patricia. *One Very, Very Quiet Afternoon*. Greenwillow, 1986.

Lobel, Arnold. *On Market Street*. Greenwillow, 1981.

Lopshire, Robert. *ABC Games*. Thomas Y. Crowell, 1986.

MacDonald, Suse. *Alphabitics*. Bradbury, 1986.

Merriam, Eve. *Good Night to Annie*. Four Winds Press, 1980.

Miller, Jane. *Farm Alphabet Book*. Prentice-Hall, 1983.

Pearson, Tracey C., ill. *A Apple Pie*. Dial, 1986.

Scarry, Richard. *Richard Scarry's A B C Word Book*. Random House, 1971.

Stevenson, James. *Grandpa's Great City Book*. Greenwillow, 1983.

Walker, Barbara. *I Packed My Trunk to Go to _____*. Follett, 1969.

Yolen, Jane. *All in the Woodland Early*. Collins-World, 1980.

POETRY & RHYMES

POETRY & RHYMES

Happiness is children chanting as they play, making up tunes and rhymes as they go. No wonder they're ready for Mother Goose and other poems! Try some of the following suggestions.

Whiskers and Rhymes
Arnold Lobel

This is a book of new nursery rhymes with a Mother Gooselike quality. Children will respond to the strong rhythm and the taste of the words on their tongues and will learn them quickly. The whimsical cat characters will spark conversations and should be good for a chuckle or two.

■ Since some of these verses imitate certain Mother Goose rhymes, children can be encouraged to create their own. Try reading "Orson, Porson, Pudding and Pie" and, just for fun, ask children to substitute other rhyming names and different nouns or actions.

■ Make a cassette record of several selections from the book with marked rhythms. Children can march, skip, or hop in time or act them out. This same or another cassette can be placed in the library corner. Children can select the appropriate pictures while rereading the book.

Tomie de Paola's Mother Goose
Tomie de Paola

De Paola's pictures bring new life to many old favorite classic nursery rhymes. He has included some verses not usually found in most collections and also some longer narratives. Children will love these wonderful pictures and enjoy saying the rhymes with you.

■ After reading many of the selections with the children, try using one of the longer rhymes like "There Was a Little Woman" and assign parts to different children to act out.

■ Assemble a box of simple props so that children can use them to pantomime favorite rhymes. Have others guess who the character is and then all say the rhyme together. Suggested rhymes to use are: *"Little Boy Blue," "Little Jack Horner," "Little Bo-peep," "Little Miss Muffet," "Jack Be Nimble," "Old King Cole," "Mistress Mary."* Then, choose a small group of children and pass the book around the circle while each child "reads" a rhyme out loud.

Wishes, Whispers and Secrets
Jane Belk Moncure

A short delightful poetic definition on one page is accompanied by a large, full-color picture on the facing page. Excellent for vocabulary development or just talking about and enjoying the pictures. Children will savor sounds like, "a bee whispers spring with a hum-buzzy buzz."

■ After reading the book aloud, ask individual children to define what the terms *wishes, whispers,* and *secrets* mean to them. Record their answers on a cassette and play it back so that everyone can hear. You may wish to write some of the definitions on a chart to be added to later on.

■ Take an invisible piece of magic chalk and draw a magic circle around a single child or a small group of children. Ask the child or group to pantomime what they would do or who they would be if they had three wishes. Have the children watching try to guess the wishes first without any verbal clues. Then, if necessary, have the wisher give clues in words. Discuss real and make-believe when necessary.

PROP BOX

★ GUESS the nursery rhyme by looking at one of the props.

★ MATCH two props from the same nursery rhyme.

★ RECREATE a nursery rhyme with actions and props.

★ MIX up the props and create a new nursery rhyme.

POETRY & RHYMES

After reading and reciting poems and Mother Goose rhymes for a few days, arrange a collection of rhyming books where children can get at them easily. You may want to introduce one or more of the following books during a group discussion time and then, place them in a special spot. When a child finds an interesting illustrated verse, take time to read it aloud.

Snowman Sniffles and Other Verses
N. M. Bodecker

This is a book of short poems—light, sometimes humorous—all of which are illustrated by fine line drawings. This book is meant to be shared.

Rhymes Around the Day
Pat Thomson

Twin sisters who are dressed in different colors are pictured in this nursery rhyme book with a modern setting. Children will find verses like "Miss Polly had a dolly who was sick, sick, sick."

Hailstones and Halibut Bones
Mary O'Neill

Children will respond to the feel and taste of the words in these poems about colors. Each color has its own poem.

Skip to My Lou
Robert Quackenbush

Each of the verses to this old folk song is accompanied here by hilarious illustrations. The choruses are great for dramatic play.

Honey, I Love
Eloise Greenfield

Warm, touching love poems and soft, lovely illustrations of black children are found throughout this book.

The Comic Adventures of Old Mother Hubbard and Her Dog
Sarah Catherine Martin

This old nursery rhyme is presented in a theatrical setting with the main characters in costume. Other familiar nursery rhyme characters can be found in the page borders.

A Light in the Attic
Shel Silverstein

This collection of zany poetry—which sometimes uncovers childhood fears—is familiar by now to many. Most of the short selections are suitable for young children.

MOTIVATORS

Here are some general "motivators" that will fit the books above and any other poetry or Mother Goose books that you have collected for your room.

1. See if you can find a book that is about just one Mother Goose rhyme.
(Mary Had a Little Lamb, Hector Protector, Old Mother Hubbard)

2. In which book can you find pictures of Little Boy Blue or Little Miss Muffet?

3. Find a Mother Goose book where the animals are dressed like people.

4. Which poetry book has your favorite poem in it?

5. Bring up the book in which you like the pictures best.

THREE LITTLE PIGS PILLOWS

YOU'LL NEED:

- ½ yd. pink cotton/poly fabric (2 layers)
- polyester stuffing
- needle/thread
- permanent markers or fabric paints/brush
- rubber bands

WHAT TO DO:

1. Cut two pieces of fabric like so:

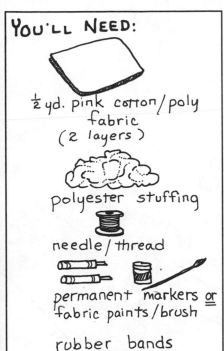

13" 15" 13"
17"

2. Sew around two pieces about ¼" in from edges. Leave 4" open in order to turn.

Clip into curved edges. Turn right side out.

open
↑ clip

3. Pull each corner together about 3" down from the points and secure with rubber bands.

rubber bands → 3" 3"

4. Cut out a 7" circle from fabric. With needle and thread, baste ¼" around edge of whole circle. Pull threads to make a sack. Stuff with polyester. Use markers to draw on nostrils on this 'snout.'

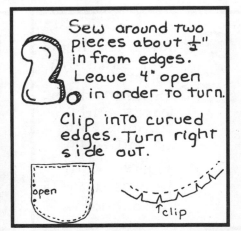

5. Use permanent markers (or fabric paint and brush) and the illustration to add facial characteristics. Stuff with polyester stuffing.

blue
brown
pink →
pink →

6. Slip stitch opening closed. Use needle and thread to sew 'snout' onto center of pig's face.

slip stitch

RHYMING STICK PUPPETS

YOU'LL NEED:

Construction paper

craft sticks (or depressors)

tape

crayons
markers

Rhyming Words

<u>man</u>: is in front of the <u>fan</u>
is hopping over a <u>can</u>
is looking at a <u>pan</u>.
is getting a <u>tan</u>.

<u>car</u>: got stuck in <u>tar</u>
stopped at a <u>bar</u>
ran over a <u>jar</u>.
got stopped by a man with a <u>star</u>.

<u>pig</u>: was dancing a <u>jig</u>
was eating a <u>fig</u>.
drove a <u>rig</u>.

<u>cat</u>: had lunch with a <u>rat</u>
took a turn at <u>bat</u>
wore a wild <u>hat</u>
warmed up the <u>mat</u>
just <u>sat</u>.

WHAT TO DO:

1. Children draw and cut out a figure or object—such as a <u>man</u>, a <u>car</u>, a <u>cat</u>, a <u>pig</u>. The figure or object is mounted on a craft stick with tape.

2. Using the figure as a starting point, have children rhyme words and actions that go with that figure. Adult records answers on a chart.

3. Have children draw illustrations to represent those words that rhyme, cut out and mount each on a craft stick.

4. Set up a stage—either a table turned on its side or a sheet half way across a doorway.

5. Children use the figures and objects to illustrate a simple rhyme...
"the man is in front of the fan" or "the pig is doing a jig"

6. Children can tell what is happening <u>or</u> have members of the audience guess and say aloud what they see happening.

THREE LITTLE PIGS PILLOWS

YOU'LL NEED:

½ yd. pink cotton/poly fabric (2 layers)

polyester stuffing

needle/thread

permanent markers or fabric paints/brush

rubber bands

WHAT TO DO:

1. Cut two pieces of fabric like so:

15"
13"   13"
17"

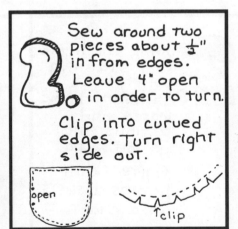

2. Sew around two pieces about ¼" in from edges. Leave 4" open in order to turn.

Clip into curved edges. Turn right side out.

open

clip

3. Pull each corner together about 3" down from the points and secure with rubber bands.

3"   3"

rubber bands →

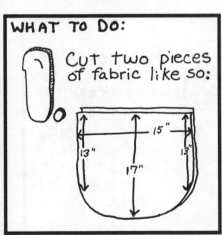

4. Cut out a 7" circle from fabric. With needle and thread, baste ¼" around edge of whole circle. Pull threads to make a sack. Stuff with polyester. Use markers to draw on nostrils on this 'snout.'

5. Use permanent markers (or fabric paint and brush) and the illustration to add facial characteristics. Stuff with polyester stuffing.

blue
brown
pink →
pink →

6. Slip stitch opening closed. Use needle and thread to sew 'snout' onto center of pig's face.

slip stitch

RHYMING STICK PUPPETS

YOU'LL NEED:

 Construction paper

 craft sticks (or depressors)

tape

 crayons markers

Rhyming Words

<u>man</u>: is in front of the <u>fan</u>
is hopping over a <u>can</u>
is looking at a <u>pan</u>.
is getting a <u>tan</u>.

<u>car</u>: got stuck in <u>tar</u>
stopped at a <u>bar</u>
ran over a <u>jar</u>.
got stopped by
a man with
a <u>star</u>.

<u>pig</u>: was dancing a <u>jig</u>
was eating a <u>fig</u>.
drove a <u>rig</u>.

<u>cat</u>: had lunch with a
<u>rat</u>
took a turn at <u>bat</u>
wore a wild <u>hat</u>
warmed up the <u>mat</u>
just <u>sat</u>.

WHAT TO DO:

 1. Children draw and cut out a figure or object—such as a <u>man</u>, a <u>car</u>, a <u>cat</u>, a <u>pig</u>. The figure or object is mounted on a craft stick with tape.

 2. Using the figure as a starting point, have children rhyme words and actions that go with that figure. Adult records answers on a chart.

3. Have children draw illustrations to represent those words that rhyme, cut out and mount each on a craft stick.

 4. Set up a stage— either a table turned on its side or a sheet half way across a doorway.

 5. Children use the figures and objects to illustrate a simple rhyme...
"the man is in front of the fan" or
"the pig is doing a jig"

 6. Children can tell what is happening <u>or</u> have members of the audience guess and say aloud what they see happening.

EASY ON / EASY OFF BOARD

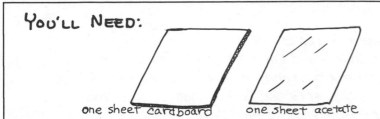

YOU'LL NEED:

one sheet cardboard

one sheet acetate

masking tape

 felt tipped MARKERS — markers

1. WHAT TO DO:
Place acetate sheet over cardboard and tape acetate onto cardboard by folding piece of masking tape over top from front to back.

2.
Place a drawn game (on a piece of plain paper) under the acetate sheet and over the cardboard.

3.
Use water soluble markers to write on acetate. Wipe acetate with a damp cloth or tissue to remove marker.

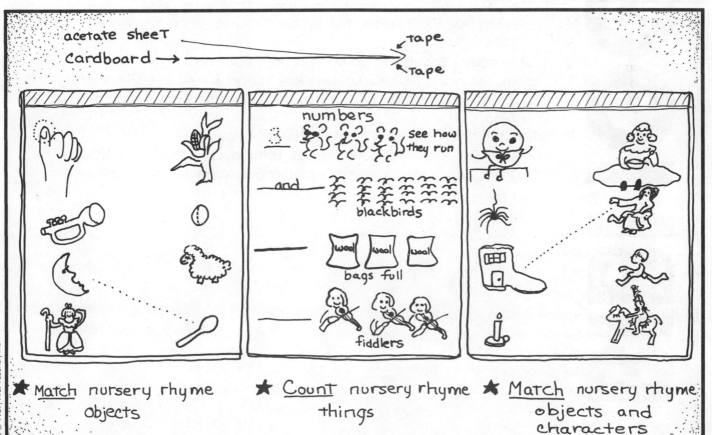

acetate sheet → tape
cardboard → Tape

numbers — see how they run
and — blackbirds
— wool wool wool — bags full
— fiddlers

★ <u>Match</u> nursery rhyme objects

★ <u>Count</u> nursery rhyme things

★ <u>Match</u> nursery rhyme objects and characters

BIBLIOGRAPHY

Adoff, Arnold. *My Black Me*. E. P. Dutton, 1974.

Bodecker, N. M. *Snowman Sniffles and Other Verses*. Atheneum, 1983.

de Paola, Tomie. *Old Mother Hubbard and Her Dog*. Harcourt, 1981.

_____ . *Tomie de Paola's Mother Goose*. G. P. Putnam's Sons, 1985.

Emberley, Barbara. *Drummer Hoff*. Prentice-Hall, 1967.

Fisher, Aileen. *Feathered Ones and Furry*. Thomas Y. Crowell, 1971.

Greenfield, Eloise. *Honey, I Love*. Thomas Y. Crowell, 1978.

Hale, Sara Josepha. *Mary Had a Little Lamb*. Holiday, 1984.

Katz, Bobbi. *Month by Month*. Random House, 1984.

Kuskin, Karla. *Dogs and Dragons, Trees and Dreams*. Harper & Row, 1980.

_____ . *Near the Window Tree*. Harper & Row, 1975.

Livingston, Myra Cohn. *O Sliver of Liver and Other Poems*. Atheneum, 1979.

_____ . *A Song I Sang to You*. Harcourt, 1984.

Lobel, Arnold. *Whiskers and Rhymes*. Greenwillow, 1985.

Martin, Sarah. *The Comic Adventures of Old Mother Hubbard and Her Dog*. Bradbury, 1968.

Moncure, Jane Belk. *Wishes, Whispers and Secrets*. Child's World, 1971.

Nerlove, Miriam. *I Made a Mistake*. Atheneum, 1985.

O'Neill, Mary. *Hailstones and Halibut Bones*. Doubleday, 1961.

Provensen, Alice and Martin. *The Mother Goose Book*. Random House, 1976.

Quackenbush, Robert. *Skip to My Lou*. Lippincott, 1975.

Sendak, Maurice. *Chicken Soup with Rice*. Harper & Row, 1962.

_____ . *Hector Protector, and As I Went Over the Water*. Harper & Row, 1965.

Silverstein, Shel. *A Light in the Attic*. Harper & Row, 1981.

Thomson, Pat. *Rhymes Around the Day*. Lothrop, Lee & Shepard, 1983.

Wildsmith, Brian. *Brian Wildsmith's Mother Goose*. Franklin Watts, 1964.

ANIMALS

ANIMALS

Animal books have always been favorites of children. From them, young people can learn either factual information about real animals or more about the way people act. Authors often ascribe human characteristics to animals and write delightful tales about how the story characters get themselves in and out of problem situations. While discussing the books and activities suggested below and in other places, you will have good opportunities to introduce the library classifications of nonfiction (realistic, factual) and fiction (make-believe) books.

Emma's Pet
David McPhail

Emma is searching for a big, soft, cuddly pet and the book shows different possibilities. Animals with their various characteristics are shown; none fit her bill. Emma's choice finally appears!
■ On each page, as the book is being read, let children discuss the animal and its characteristics. Have them decide if Emma will pick it and explain their reasons.
■ On a lapboard, show a few toy or stuffed animals and ask a child to use two or three descriptive words to tell about one of them. Have the rest of the group decide which animal fits the description.

What's That Noise?
Michele Lemieux

Brown Bear tries to find a noise that he hears as he looks at other animals, birds, and people. He listens to the sounds they make. The noise turns out to be his own heart getting ready for a long winter nap.
■ Read the story. Ask children to think of some words that are used to describe sounds that the animals make.
■ Have each child choose and act out an animal whose sounds and movements can be imitated. Have others identify it.

Whose Footprints
Masayuki Yabuuchi

On separate pages, children see footprints or hoofprints and are asked to identify the animal to whom they belong. The appropriate animal is shown on the following page.
■ As the book is being shown to the group, let children talk about the appearance of a set of prints using their own vocabulary and then guess which animal's feet have been depicted and described.
■ Bring in props, such as a jelly roll pan and wet sand, or have the group stand around the sand table. Let a child choose a toy or stuffed animal in the room and make a paw or footprint while the rest have their eyes closed. Then, ask children to identify what made the print.

Deep in the Forest
Brinton Turkle

In the reverse of the traditional story, "Goldilocks and the Three Bears," one of the bears visits Goldilocks' house.
■ Read the story and then find out if children realize the similarity between this story and the old familiar one. Ask children to retell "Goldilocks and the Three Bears." Let them compare the two stories.
■ Use dramatic play furniture and dishes, and have children role play both of the versions.

LOOK AGAIN

 TURN THE PAGE

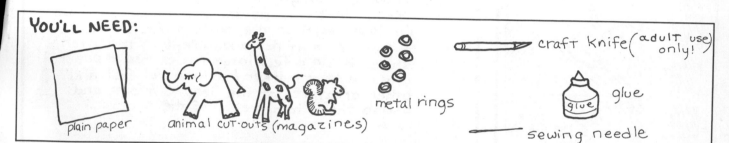

YOU'LL NEED:

plain paper

animal cut-outs (magazines)

metal rings

craft knife (adult use only!)

glue

sewing needle

WHAT TO DO:

1. Children and adults cut out interesting pictures from magazines and mount on a piece of paper. Glue in place.

2. Place a plain piece of paper underneath mounted picture paper. Use pin to make four dots (in shape of square or rectangle) on highlighted part.

3. Four dots will show up on plain paper and when connected, form a "window". Cut open "window" with craft knife.

←CUT

4. Place paper, with cut-out window, over mounted picture paper so that just a curious piece of the picture shows.

5. Make a few mounted pictures and corresponding "window" pages. Bind together to form a book.

6. Children look at "window" page and see small part of animal showing through. Child guesses what animal and checks by turning page.

FOOTPRINTS

YOU'LL NEED:

inner tire tube rubber

scissors

glue

 scrap wood

WHAT TO DO:

1. Adult makes stamps by cutting inner tire tube rubber into the shape of an animal track. (See samples.) Also, be sure to include a human foot!

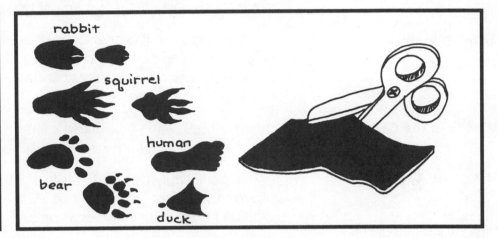

rabbit

squirrel

human

bear

duck

2. The two or four cut-out tracks or prints are glued onto a scrap of wood or thick cardboard. Allow each stamp to dry overnight.

GLUE

3. Use 'footprint' stamps to make mazes with tracks leading from woods to a home for that particular animal. Make matching track games and decorate stationary.

Stephen

ANIMALS

Animal books can help children learn facts, discuss humanlike characteristics as portrayed by certain animals, or just have fun. You may want to include a mixture of types so that the differences will be more evident to children as you introduce some of the following books. Then, place the books in the library corner or on your science table.

A Snake Is Totally Tail
Judi Barrett

The important characteristics of various animals are depicted in clever ways and described humorously and alliteratively. After reading the title, see if children can figure out any of the "word pictures."

Trouble in the Ark
Gerald Rose

Here children will hear and "see" onomatopoetic words that demonstrate how different animals sound as they talk. The artist has used unusual calligraphy when printing the sound words; thus, children can guess more easily what the sounds will be.

What's in the Cave?
Peter Seymour

In this book with lift-up flaps, children find out about the types of animals and their homes that are located in this cave.

Have You Seen My Cat?
Eric Carle

This book easily demonstrates through its illustrations the different types of animals that can belong to one "family" including those that children wouldn't keep in their homes as pets.

Annie and the Wild Animals
Jan Brett

Annie is not able to find her pet so she tries to pick a new one from some really unsuitable woodland animals. In the border, children see a second story, one dealing with her pet cat, taking place.

Animals Made by Me
Margery W. Brown

A boy finds some magic chalk and starts adding details to animals so that they are funny-looking and unusual.

Curious George Visits the Zoo
Margaret Rey

Children's favorite monkey goes to the zoo to see what animals are there and learns how to describe the residents.

Have You Seen My Duckling?
Nancy Tafuri

A mother duck and her family go out for a swim and according to her, one small duckling is missing. The readers know this isn't true—the little web-footed bird can be seen hiding in places in or near the pond.

MOTIVATORS

Try some of these general motivators to help stimulate children into further book explorations. Let them try to classify what is found on your shelves into real and fantasy books about animals. If detailed questions are asked about specific books, children will learn more about different animal categories.

1. Find a book that shows photographs of real animals.
2. Find a book that shows animals that look funny or may be make-believe.
3. Discover a book that has pictures of where different animals live.
4. Find a book where animals are doing the same things that people do.
5. Bring me a book that shows your favorite animal and we will read it.

environments

YOU'LL NEED: cardboard boxes, plastic wrap, clay, plants, string, sand, soil, pebbles, shells, twigs

WHAT TO DO:

IN THE OCEAN

1. Prepare a large carton to look like an ocean. Paint the insides of it blue. Put sand (or table salt) on the bottom. Add shells if possible, or if not available, use macaroni shells. Put in a few large rocks. Then, on paper, draw, paint or marker big, colorful fish and other creatures of the deep. Cut out and string them from the top of the carton.

IN THE DESERT

2. Create a desert terrarium. Use real cactus plants set in soil and sand. (Children could also cut cactus plants from green construction paper or chunks of styrofoam) Use small pebbles to make desert inhabitants, such as lizards and prairie dogs. Play dough can make a snake or bird. Set all this in a pie plate or cardboard box lined with plastic wrap.

IN THE FOREST

3. Recreate a woodland environment in which children can play. Add to a sand area or sand pile: branches (trees); small twigs (to build nests); large boxes covered with sand (they become caves); a hole in the sand lined with plastic (pond); mud and twigs (beaver dam). Add child-made clay squirrels, robins, beavers, bears, ducks, and snakes.

CREATE·A·CLAY ANIMAL

an elephiraffe or a giraffephant ?

YOU'LL NEED:

plasticene
(This will stay soft)

or

water base clay
(This dries hard and can be kiln fired)

WHAT TO DO:

1. Two children sit together, facing each other. Each has a large lump of clay.

2. Each child thinks of an animal but does not tell the other person what it is.

3. One child shapes a piece of clay into one part of the body of the animal that he is thinking of.

4. The other child shapes a piece of clay into one part of the animal he has thought of and <u>adds</u> it to the first piece.

5. The children alternate turns, adding <u>their</u> animal body part to only the one animal. (Remind them that only one head is needed)

6. Children complete animal and guess what each is. Give the newly created animal a name!

93

BIBLIOGRAPHY

Arnosky, Jim. *Deer at the Brook*. Lothrop, Lee & Shepard, 1986.

Asbjornsen, Peter. *The Three Billy Goats Gruff*. Seabury, 1973.

Balian, Lorna. *Amelia's Nine Lives*. Abingdon, 1986.

Barrett, Judi. *A Snake Is Totally Tail*. Atheneum, 1983.

Brandenberg, Franz. *Otto Is Different*. Greenwillow, 1985.

Brett, Jan. Annie and the Wild Animals. Houghton Mifflin, 1985.

Brown, Margery. *Animals Made by Me*. G. P. Putnam's Sons, 1970.

Carle, Eric. *Have You Seen My Cat?*. Franklin Watts, 1973.

_____. *The Mixed-Up Chameleon*. Thomas Y. Crowell, 1984.

Cleary, Beverly. *Two Dog Biscuits*. Wm. Morrow, 1985.

Foreman, Michael. *Cat and Canary*. E. P. Dutton, 1985.

Hawkins, Colin and Jacqui. *Farmyard Sounds*. G. P. Putnam's Sons, 1985.

Heller, Ruth. *How to Hide a Butterfly and Other Insects*. Grosset and Dunlap, 1985.

Hoban, Tana. *A Children's Zoo*. Greenwillow, 1985.

Lane, Margaret. *The Elephant*. Random House, 1985.

_____. *The Giraffe*. Random House, 1985.

_____. *The Lion*. Random House, 1985.

Leford, Byou. *Good Wood Bear*. Bradbury, 1985.

Lemieux, Michele. *What's That Noise?* Wm. Morrow, 1984.

Lester, Helen. *A Porcupine Named Fluffy*. Houghton Mifflin, 1986.

McPhail, David. *Emma's Pet*. E. P. Dutton, 1985.

Price, Matthew and Sue Porter. *Do You See What I See?*. Harper & Row, 1986.

Rey, Margaret. *Curious George Visits the Zoo*. Houghton Mifflin, 1985.

Rockwell, Anne. *The Three Bears and 15 Other Stories*. Crown, 1975.

Rose, Anne. *Akimba and the Magic Cow*. Four Winds, 1979.

Rose, Gerald. *Trouble in the Ark*. Bodley Head, 1985.

Seymour, Peter. *What's in the Cave?*. Holt, Rinehart & Winston, 1985.

Tafuri, Nancy. *Have You Seen My Duckling?*. Greenwillow, 1984.

_____. *Rabbit's Morning*. Greenwillow, 1985.

Testa, Fulvio. *Wolf's Favor*. Dial, 1986.

Turkle, Brinton. *Deep in the Forest*. E. P. Dutton, 1976.

White, Nancy. *Jesse Bear, What Will You Wear?*. Carlstrom, 1986.

Yabuuchi, Masayuki. *Whose Footprints*. Philomel, 1985.

FEELINGS

FEELINGS

The children in our care are learning to cope with a variety of emotions ranging from anxiety and fear to love, jealousy, and anger. Talking about what book characters do and feel in similar situations can help children verbalize their own situations and will help us in turn to understand them as we help them mature. The books and suggestions below are just a sampling of those available to you.

Martha's Mad Day
Miranda Hapgood

Martha, in a mean, fierce mood, wakes up and throws Pig across the room, dumps breakfast on the floor, and spends the rest of the day pretending to be queen and having everyone obey her. At bedtime, it's a different story, however.
■ Discuss anger with children. Have them tell some of the things that make them angry and how they feel when others are angry. Discuss ways of getting rid of anger that do not hurt anyone.
■ Using masks or sock puppets, have children act out "angry" situations.

A Special Trade
Sally Wittman

Bartholomew, a grandfather figure, is little Nelly's neighbor and takes her everywhere in her stroller. As they both grow older, things change and Nelly lovingly pushes Bartholomew in his wheelchair.
■ Show children some of the pictures first. Ask them to tell what they would like to know about each character. After showing only the first half of the pages, see if they can predict the outcome of the story.
■ Talk about grandparents or other senior citizens in the children's lives. Ask, "What are some of the fun things you all do together? How can children help care for older people?"

Cousins Are Special
Susan Goldman

Sarah visits Carol Sue and the two of them have a wonderful time getting into all kinds of mischief. When they discover that they both have the same grandmother, they realize that "cousin love" is special.
■ Set up the dramatic play area to look like Auntie's house. Have children take turns packing a suitcase and going to visit.
■ This is a perfect opportunity to discuss family visits and things children would like to do or have done with cousins. Ask each child to think of one special thing about a cousin—or a friend.

When the New Baby Comes, I'm Moving Out
Martha Alexander

Oliver tells his mother exactly how he feels about the fact that she's redoing all his things for the new baby. His mother is very reassuring and tells him all the reasons she needs him.
■ This is a good time to discuss how life at home can change while waiting for a new baby and after it arrives.
■ The dramatic play area can be set up with a supply of bottles, make-believe baby food, and disposable diapers. Children can be encouraged to take turns role-playing Baby, Mom, Dad, themselves, a neighbor, or older relative. You might ask some "what if" questions here, such as, "What if the baby cries a lot and Mom isn't there for a minute?"

FOOTPRINTS

YOU'LL NEED:

inner tire tube rubber

 scissors

 glue

 scrap wood

WHAT TO DO:

1. Adult makes stamps by cutting inner tire tube rubber into the shape of an animal track. (See Samples.) Also be sure to include a human foot!

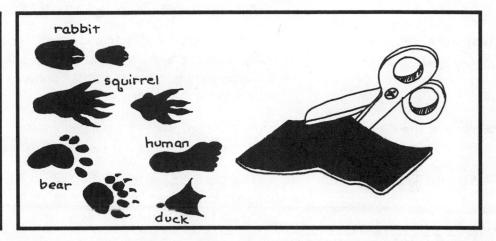

rabbit

squirrel

human

bear

duck

2. The two or four cut-out tracks or prints are glued onto a scrap of wood or thick cardboard. Allow each stamp to dry overnight.

3. Use 'footprint' stamps to make mazes with tracks leading from woods to a home for that particular animal. Make matching track games and decorate stationary.

Stephen

89

ANIMALS

Animal books can help children learn facts, discuss humanlike characteristics as portrayed by certain animals, or just have fun. You may want to include a mixture of types so that the differences will be more evident to children as you introduce some of the following books. Then, place the books in the library corner or on your science table.

A Snake Is Totally Tail
Judi Barrett

The important characteristics of various animals are depicted in clever ways and described humorously and alliteratively. After reading the title, see if children can figure out any of the "word pictures."

Trouble in the Ark
Gerald Rose

Here children will hear and "see" onomatopoetic words that demonstrate how different animals sound as they talk. The artist has used unusual calligraphy when printing the sound words; thus, children can guess more easily what the sounds will be.

What's in the Cave?
Peter Seymour

In this book with lift-up flaps, children find out about the types of animals and their homes that are located in this cave.

Have You Seen My Cat?
Eric Carle

This book easily demonstrates through its illustrations the different types of animals that can belong to one "family" including those that children wouldn't keep in their homes as pets.

Annie and the Wild Animals
Jan Brett

Annie is not able to find her pet so she tries to pick a new one from some really unsuitable woodland animals. In the border, children see a second story, one dealing with her pet cat, taking place.

Animals Made by Me
Margery W. Brown

A boy finds some magic chalk and starts adding details to animals so that they are funny-looking and unusual.

Curious George Visits the Zoo
Margaret Rey

Children's favorite monkey goes to the zoo to see what animals are there and learns how to describe the residents.

Have You Seen My Duckling?
Nancy Tafuri

A mother duck and her family go out for a swim and according to her, one small duckling is missing. The readers know this isn't true—the little web-footed bird can be seen hiding in places in or near the pond.

MOTIVATORS

Try some of these general motivators to help stimulate children into further book explorations. Let them try to classify what is found on your shelves into real and fantasy books about animals. If detailed questions are asked about specific books, children will learn more about different animal categories.
1. Find a book that shows photographs of real animals.
2. Find a book that shows animals that look funny or may be make-believe.
3. Discover a book that has pictures of where different animals live.
4. Find a book where animals are doing the same things that people do.
5. Bring me a book that shows your favorite animal and we will read it.

environments

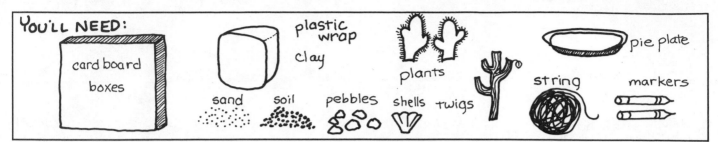

YOU'LL NEED: card board boxes · plastic wrap · clay · plants · pie plate · sand · soil · pebbles · shells · twigs · string · markers

WHAT TO DO:

IN THE OCEAN

1. Prepare a large carton to look like an ocean. Paint the insides of it blue. Put sand (or table salt) on the bottom. Add shells if possible, or if not available, use macaroni shells. Put in a few large rocks. Then, on paper, draw, paint or marker big, colorful fish and other creatures of the deep. Cut out and string them from the top of the carton.

IN THE DESERT

2. Create a desert terrarium. Use real cactus plants set in soil and sand. (Children could also cut cactus plants from green construction paper or chunks of styrofoam) Use small pebbles to make desert inhabitants, such as lizards and praire dogs. Play dough can make a snake or bird. Set all this in a pie plate or cardboard box lined with plastic wrap.

IN THE FOREST

3. Recreate a woodland environment in which children can play. Add to a sand area or sand pile: branches (trees); small twigs (to build nests); large boxes covered with sand (they become caves); a hole in the sand lined with plastic (pond); mud and twigs (beaver dam). Add child-made clay squirrels, robins, beavers, bears, ducks, and snakes.

LOOK AGAIN

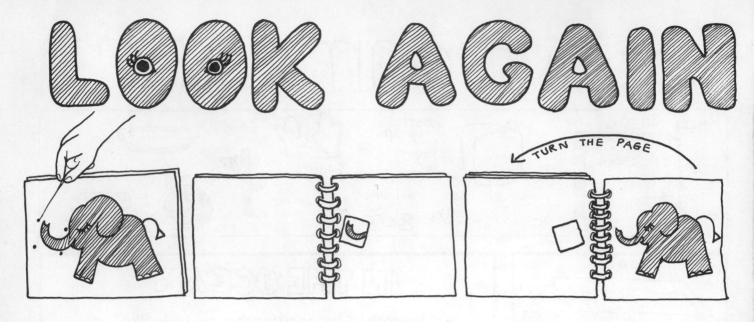

TURN THE PAGE

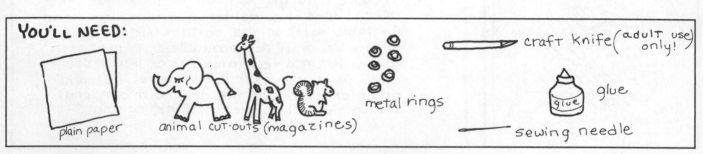

YOU'LL NEED:

plain paper

animal cut-outs (magazines)

metal rings

craft knife (adult use only!)

glue

sewing needle

WHAT to DO:

1. Children and adults cut out interesting pictures from magazines and mount on a piece of paper. Glue in place.

2. Place a plain piece of paper underneath mounted picture paper. Use pin to make four dots (in shape of square or rectangle) on highlighted part.

3. Four dots will show up on plain paper and when connected, form a "window". Cut open "window" with craft knife. ←CUT

4. Place paper, with cut-out window, over mounted picture paper so that just a curious piece of the picture shows.

5. Make a few mounted pictures and corresponding "window" pages. Bind together to form a book.

6. Children look at "window" page and see small part of animal showing through. Child guesses what animal and checks by turning page.

CREATE·A·CLAY ANIMAL

an elephiraffe or
a giraffephant?

YOU'LL NEED:

plasticene   or   water base clay
(This will stay soft)   (This dries hard
                          and can be
                          kiln fired)

WHAT TO DO:

1. Two children sit together, facing each other. Each has a large lump of clay.

2. Each child thinks of an animal but does not tell the other person what it is.

3. One child shapes a piece of clay into one part of the body of the animal that he is thinking of.

4. The other child shapes a piece of clay into one part of the animal he has thought of and <u>adds</u> it to the first piece.

5. The children alternate turns, adding <u>their</u> animal body part to only the one animal. (Remind them that only one head is needed)

6. Children complete animal and guess what each is. Give the newly created animal a name!

93

BIBLIOGRAPHY

Arnosky, Jim. *Deer at the Brook*. Lothrop, Lee & Shepard, 1986.

Asbjornsen, Peter. *The Three Billy Goats Gruff*. Seabury, 1973.

Balian, Lorna. *Amelia's Nine Lives*. Abingdon, 1986.

Barrett, Judi. *A Snake Is Totally Tail*. Atheneum, 1983.

Brandenberg, Franz. *Otto Is Different. Greenwillow, 1985*.

Brett, Jan. Annie and the Wild Animals. Houghton Mifflin, 1985.

Brown, Margery. *Animals Made by Me*. G. P. Putnam's Sons, 1970.

Carle, Eric. *Have You Seen My Cat?*. Franklin Watts, 1973.

_____ . *The Mixed-Up Chameleon*. Thomas Y. Crowell, 1984.

Cleary, Beverly. *Two Dog Biscuits*. Wm. Morrow, 1985.

Foreman, Michael. *Cat and Canary*. E. P. Dutton, 1985.

Hawkins, Colin and Jacqui. *Farmyard Sounds*. G. P. Putnam's Sons, 1985.

Heller, Ruth. *How to Hide a Butterfly and Other Insects*. Grosset and
    Dunlap, 1985.

Hoban, Tana. *A Children's Zoo*. Greenwillow, 1985.

Lane, Margaret. *The Elephant*. Random House, 1985.

_____ . *The Giraffe*. Random House, 1985.

_____ . *The Lion*. Random House, 1985.

Leford, Byou. *Good Wood Bear*. Bradbury, 1985.

Lemieux, Michele. *What's That Noise?* Wm. Morrow, 1984.

Lester, Helen. *A Porcupine Named Fluffy*. Houghton Mifflin, 1986.

McPhail, David. *Emma's Pet*. E. P. Dutton, 1985.

Price, Matthew and Sue Porter. *Do You See What I See?*. Harper & Row,
    1986.

Rey, Margaret. *Curious George Visits the Zoo*. Houghton Mifflin, 1985.

Rockwell, Anne. *The Three Bears and 15 Other Stories*. Crown, 1975.

Rose, Anne. *Akimba and the Magic Cow*. Four Winds, 1979.

Rose, Gerald. *Trouble in the Ark*. Bodley Head, 1985.

Seymour, Peter. *What's in the Cave?*. Holt, Rinehart & Winston, 1985.

Tafuri, Nancy. *Have You Seen My Duckling?*. Greenwillow, 1984.

_____ . *Rabbit's Morning*. Greenwillow, 1985.

Testa, Fulvio. *Wolf's Favor*. Dial, 1986.

Turkle, Brinton. *Deep in the Forest*. E. P. Dutton, 1976.

White, Nancy. *Jesse Bear, What Will You Wear?*. Carlstrom, 1986.

Yabuuchi, Masayuki. *Whose Footprints*. Philomel, 1985.

FEELINGS

FEELINGS

The children in our care are learning to cope with a variety of emotions ranging from anxiety and fear to love, jealousy, and anger. Talking about what book characters do and feel in similar situations can help children verbalize their own situations and will help us in turn to understand them as we help them mature. The books and suggestions below are just a sampling of those available to you.

Martha's Mad Day
Miranda Hapgood

Martha, in a mean, fierce mood, wakes up and throws Pig across the room, dumps breakfast on the floor, and spends the rest of the day pretending to be queen and having everyone obey her. At bedtime, it's a different story, however.
■ Discuss anger with children. Have them tell some of the things that make them angry and how they feel when others are angry. Discuss ways of getting rid of anger that do not hurt anyone.
■ Using masks or sock puppets, have children act out "angry" situations.

A Special Trade
Sally Wittman

Bartholomew, a grandfather figure, is little Nelly's neighbor and takes her everywhere in her stroller. As they both grow older, things change and Nelly lovingly pushes Bartholomew in his wheelchair.
■ Show children some of the pictures first. Ask them to tell what they would like to know about each character. After showing only the first half of the pages, see if they can predict the outcome of the story.
■ Talk about grandparents or other senior citizens in the children's lives. Ask, "What are some of the fun things you all do together? How can children help care for older people?"

Cousins Are Special
Susan Goldman

Sarah visits Carol Sue and the two of them have a wonderful time getting into all kinds of mischief. When they discover that they both have the same grandmother, they realize that "cousin love" is special.
■ Set up the dramatic play area to look like Auntie's house. Have children take turns packing a suitcase and going to visit.
■ This is a perfect opportunity to discuss family visits and things children would like to do or have done with cousins. Ask each child to think of one special thing about a cousin—or a friend.

When the New Baby Comes, I'm Moving Out
Martha Alexander

Oliver tells his mother exactly how he feels about the fact that she's redoing all his things for the new baby. His mother is very reassuring and tells him all the reasons she needs him.
■ This is a good time to discuss how life at home can change while waiting for a new baby and after it arrives.
■ The dramatic play area can be set up with a supply of bottles, make-believe baby food, and disposable diapers. Children can be encouraged to take turns role-playing Baby, Mom, Dad, themselves, a neighbor, or older relative. You might ask some "what if" questions here, such as, "What if the baby cries a lot and Mom isn't there for a minute?"

MASKS

sleepy happy sad surprised angry scared

YOU'LL NEED:

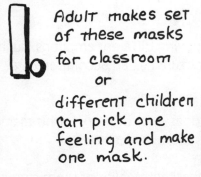 six paper plates

tongue depressors or craft sticks

Tape

markers

craft knife

WHAT TO DO:

1. Adult makes set of these masks for classroom or different children can pick one feeling and make one mask.

2. Use markers and copy each expression from above onto each paper plate.

3. Adult uses craft knife to cut out eye holes for child to see through mask.

4. Attach tongue depressor or craft stick to bottom of mask with tape.

5. Children can use masks to discuss feelings and reactions to 'real-life' situations and role playing.

6. Children can tell a story or illustrate one you read by using the appropriate masks.

FEELINGS

You may wish to assemble some titles all based on a single emotion, such as love or perhaps jealousy, or you may want to have a more varied collection. Whichever way you choose to go, be sure to allow children amply opportunity to investigate the books.

Let's Talk About Whining
Joy Witt Berry

This book is for teacher, Mom, Dad, and the children. Reading it with them will help children better understand and perhaps modify their behavior. It will also help them understand their own and other people's feelings.

Don't You Remember?
Lucille Clifton

Four-year-old Desire Mary Tate remembers everything, but her family doesn't. She expresses her emotions in different ways, including being angry.

Are You Sad, Mama?
Elizabeth Winthrop

The little girl's mother is sad and no matter what the girl does, she can't cheer her mother up. Finally, she finds a way. This book is more fun if you clip a piece of colored construction paper over the last page so children can't see it and you let them guess the ending before they see the conclusion.

The Alligator Under the Bed
Jean Lowery Nixon

Jill thinks there's an alligator under her bed and she can't get to sleep. Her mother and father don't believe her, but Uncle Harry comes to the rescue.

I Feel
George Ancona

This book of photos shows children portraying different emotions, such as happy, shy, and lonely. Each beautiful picture has an accompanying word description next to it.

Send Wendell
Genevieve Gray

Wendell is six and lives in a project and does a lot of work for his mama because his brothers and sisters are always too busy to help.

Christmas Moon
Denys Cazet

Children will respond to the magical luminescent quality of the pictures and empathize with Patrick who can't sleep because he's sad as he remembers Grandpa.

MOTIVATORS

Here are some suggestions you may want to use to motivate children toward looking at the books and discovering new insights about people's emotions.

1. Which book can you find that shows angry children?

2. Find a book that tells about having a new baby in the house.

3. Find a book that has pictures of children who look like they are happy.

4. How do you feel right now? Find a book that shows a child with the same feeling and we'll read it together.

QUIET CORNERS

YOU'LL NEED:

a large
cardboard
carton for each child

polyester stuffing

two pieces fabric

markers

paints brush

needle
thread
scissors

WHAT TO DO:

1. Adult cuts top and one side out of a large corrugated box.

2. Child and adult makes a cushion from two pieces of fabric to fit inside box bottom.

3. Children use markers or paints to design sides of box with their names and 'favorite' things

FEELINGS FOLLOW-UP

YOU'LL NEED:

drawing paper

black construction paper

books — "I KNOW A LOT OF THINGS" "THERE'S A NIGHTMARE IN MY CLOSET" "ALEXANDER AND THE TERRIBLE..." by Jodith Viorst — Alexander and the Terrible, Horrible, No Good, Very Bad Day

scissors

tape

metal book rings

light (in lamp-ok.)

WHAT TO DO:

1. Adult reads, "Alexander and the Terrible, Horrible, No Good, Very Bad Day", to children. Discuss days that you've had that have been like Alexander's. Children draw illustrations of what happened to them, you can label. Bind all illustrations into a book "The Terrible, Horrible... etc. Book" — Reread on a bad day!

I fell off my tricycle but I was O.K.

I got lost in a store but mom found me.

THE TERRIBLE, HORRIBLE, NO GOOD, VERY BAD DAY BOOK

---

2. Adult reads, "There's a Nightmare in My Closet" to children. Children then illustrate their own 'nightmares' — in the book's manner. Take another sheet of paper. Children decorate it like a closet door cut so it opens and places the 'nightmare' behind it!

1. Draw a 'nightmare'
★ by Mercer Mayer

2. Draw a door. Cut door open on 3 sides and fold back on 4th.

3. Tape 'nightmare' picture behind door. Close door. Tape it.

---

3. Adult reads "I Know a Lot of Things" (or a similar book) to children. Discuss all the wonderful accomplishments each has done. Make black paper silhouettes, hang on the walls. Children can draw illustrations of things they know or can do and hang inside silhouette.

★ by Ann and Paul Rand

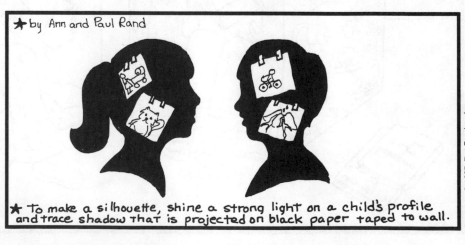

★ To make a silhouette, shine a strong light on a child's profile and trace shadow that is projected on black paper taped to wall.

FEELINGS GAME

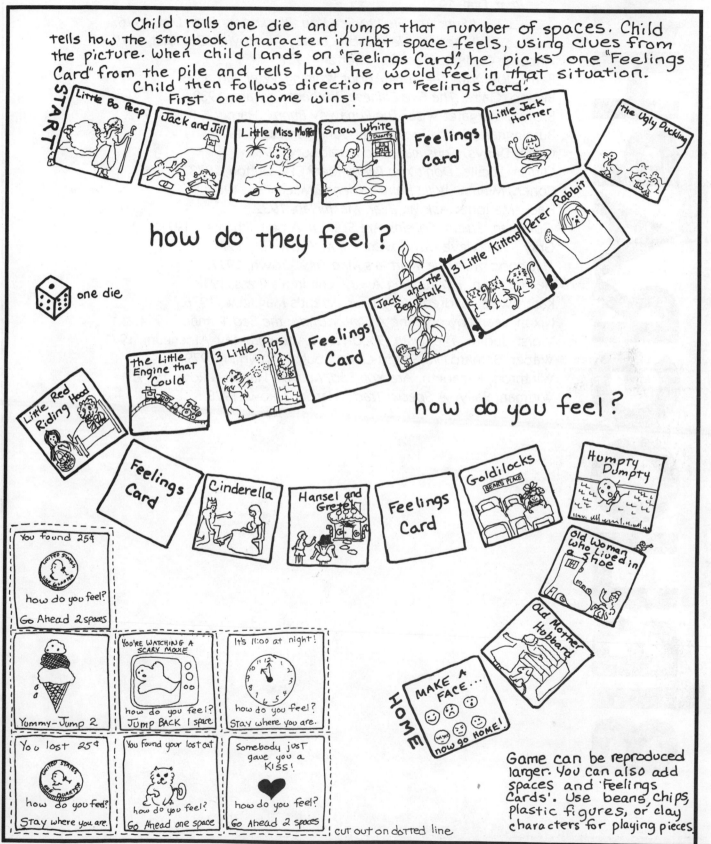

Child rolls one die and jumps that number of spaces. Child tells how the storybook character in that space feels, using clues from the picture. When child lands on "Feelings Card", he picks one "Feelings Card" from the pile and tells how he would feel in that situation. Child then follows direction on "Feelings Card". First one home wins!

START

Little Bo Peep

Jack and Jill

Little Miss Muffet

Snow White

Feelings Card

Little Jack Horner

the Ugly Duckling

how do they feel?

one die

Peter Rabbit

3 Little Kittens

Jack and the Beanstalk

Feelings Card

3 Little Pigs

the Little Engine that Could

Little Red Riding Hood

how do you feel?

Feelings Card

Cinderella

Hansel and Gretel

Feelings Card

Goldilocks
BEARS PLACE

Humpty Dumpty

Old Woman Who Lived in a Shoe

Old Mother Hubbard

MAKE A FACE...
now go HOME!

HOME

You found 25¢
UNITED STATES LIBERTY QUARTER
how do you feel?
Go Ahead 2 spaces

Yummy-Jump 2

You're watching a scary movie
how do you feel?
JUMP BACK 1 space

It's 11:00 at night!
how do you feel?
Stay where you are.

You lost 25¢
UNITED STATES LIBERTY QUARTER
how do you feel?
Stay where you are.

You found your lost cat
how do you feel?
Go Ahead one space

Somebody just gave you a KISS!
how do you feel?
Go Ahead 2 spaces

cut out on dotted line

Game can be reproduced larger. You can also add spaces and 'Feelings Cards'. Use beans, chips, plastic figures, or clay characters for playing pieces.

BIBLIOGRAPHY

Alexander, Martha. *And My Mean Old Mother Will Be Sorry, Blackboard Bear*. Dial, 1972.

_____ . *I Sure Am Glad to See You, Blackboard Bear*. Dial, 1976.

_____ . *When the New Baby Comes, I'm Moving Out*. Dial, 1979.

Ancona, George. *I Feel*. E. P. Dutton, 1977.

Berry, Joy Witt. *Let's Talk About Whining*. Peter Pan, 1982.

Bishop, Claire. *The Five Chinese Brothers*. Coward, 1938.

Brown, Margaret Wise. *The Runaway Bunny*. Harper & Row, 1942.

Burningham, John. *The Blanket*. Jonathan Cape, 1975.

Cazet, Denys. *Christmas Moon*. Bradbury, 1984.

Clifton, Lucille. *Don't You Remember?* E. P. Dutton, 1973.

Cohen, Miriam. *Will I Have a Friend?* Macmillan, 1967.

Flack, Marjorie. *Ask Mr. Bear. Macmillan, 1932.*

Goldman, Susan. Cousins Are Special. Albert Whitman, 1978.

Gray, Genevieve. *Send Wendell. McGraw-Hill, 1974.*

Hapgood, Miranda. Martha's Mad Day. Crown, 1977.

Helena, Ann. *I'm Running Away*. Children's Press, 1978.

Kantrowitz, Mildred. *Willy Bear*. Parent's Magazine, 1976.

Nixon, Jean Lowery. *The Alligator Under the Bed*. Putnam, 1974.

Viorst, Judith. *The Tenth Good Thing About Barney*. Atheneum, 1971.

Waber, Bernard. *Ira Sleeps Over*. Houghton Mifflin, 1972.

Winthrop, Elizabeth. *Are You Sad, Mama?*. Harper & Row, 1979.

Wittman, Sally. *A Special Trade*. Harper & Row, 1978.

COMMUNITY HELPERS

COMMUNITY HELPERS

As children leave home and go to school, stores, and other parts of their town, they interact with new places and people. Their worlds have broadened. Books can help them bridge gaps and learn more about their neighborhoods, the larger community in which their small worlds exist. They also learn about the special people who are a part of these new places.

City/Country
Ken Robbins

The photographs in this book show both city and country views as seen from the backseat of a car—the usual viewing place of a child.
■ Show the pictures and let children make comparisons between them and the community in which they live. Have them describe what is similar to their area and what is different.
■ Let children think about the different jobs that might need to be done in the places where the pictures were taken. Ask them to role play some of the workers at their jobs.

People Working
Douglas Florian

Here children can see people working in all different places—city, farm, on the water, offices, up in the air, underground.
■ Let children choose a page and talk about the workers and what they are doing. Encourage them to discuss any tools or machines that are being used. Point out those workers that are using their hands.
■ Ask children what objects in the room are similar to those they see on the pages in the book. Let them role play with props some of the workers they see. Have them explain how each job is done.

Maybe You Should Fly a Jet!
Theo LeSeig

In simple verse, a number of career choices are presented to children. Other occupations are also pictured and labeled.
■ Let children answer the question asked in the book, "What DO you want to do?" by miming what they would have to do at their career choices. Give individual children turns and let the rest of the group guess the job.
■ Show illustrations from the book and let children tell what they like about some of the different careers depicted. Encourage them to explain where the workers go to do their jobs. If parents of the children have similar careers, let the children tell more about those jobs.

Look Around and Listen
Joy Troth Friedman

This book concentrates on the sounds one hears in many different places, but its full illustrations give detailed pictures of many different places in a community—school, street, zoo, stores, and so on.
■ After the story has been read, let children identify different details in each picture. Help them explain in words or actions how different machines or tools work or what the people are doing.
■ Have children decide which of the places, illustrated in the book, they might be able to see in their own town. Ask them how they could "make" one of the places in their classroom. Provide time for dramatic play.

HATS

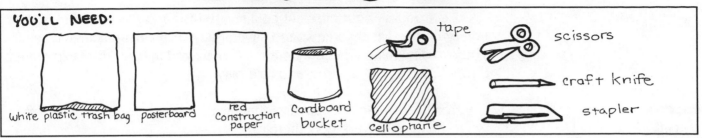

YOU'LL NEED:

White plastic trash bag · posterboard · red construction paper · cardboard bucket · cellophane · tape · scissors · craft knife · stapler

WHAT TO DO:

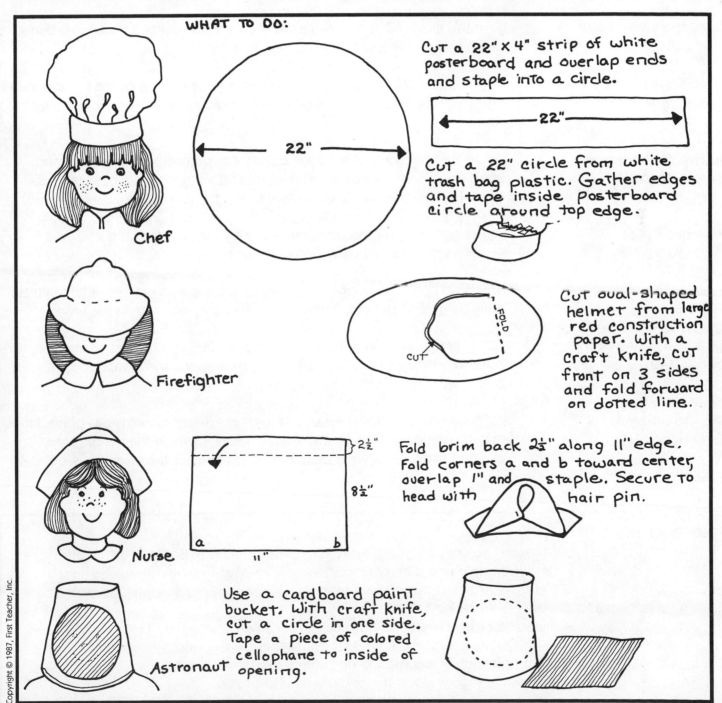

Chef — Cut a 22" x 4" strip of white posterboard and overlap ends and staple into a circle.

22"

Cut a 22" circle from white trash bag plastic. Gather edges and tape inside posterboard circle around top edge.

Firefighter — Cut oval-shaped helmet from large red construction paper. With a craft knife, cut front on 3 sides and fold forward on dotted line.

CUT · FOLD

Nurse — Fold brim back 2½" along 11" edge. Fold corners a and b toward center, overlap 1" and staple. Secure to head with hair pin.

2½" · 8½" · 11" · a · b

Astronaut — Use a cardboard paint bucket. With craft knife, cut a circle in one side. Tape a piece of colored cellophane to inside of opening.

COMMUNITY HELPERS

Collect books about different community jobs and places to put in the library corner. Let children spend several days examining them and see if you can determine what they are most interested in for further exploration through books, discussions, and role playing.

Department Store
Gail Gibbons

Here children can see activities that take place in a store and find out what the people who work there do.

Grandpa's City Book
James Stevenson

In this city ABC book, each page is covered with items found in urban settings that start with the letter being discussed.

I Can Be A Police Officer
Catherine Matthais

This books starts with a picture dictionary concerning police life and then shows with photos different tasks that a police officer is expected to learn to do.

A Visit to the Sesame Street Hospital
Deborah Hautzig

Children have a chance to see different departments in a hospital and learn about staff members and their jobs. (This helps make hospitals less scary for those who may be visiting one in the future.)

Walking Shoes
Anne Rockwell

Through this fairy tale, children may begin to realize that homes and families are important parts of a community.

Fireman Jim
Roger Bester

Through photos and the text, children see the many tasks that fire fighters must be able to perform and the tools that they need to do the work.

Girls Can be Anything
Norma Klein

The emphasis is on different jobs and the fact that females can do the same work that males do. Some of the professions shown are doctors, pilots, and presidents.

Dig, Drill, Dump, Fill
Tana Hoban

This wordless book is full of photographs that show all types of machines that children might see on the streets of their town. In the descriptions, children can discuss what people must do to make the machines work.

MOTIVATORS

Try some of these "motivators" to entice children to do further delve into the books in the library corner.

1. Which book shows lots of people doing different jobs?

2. Find a book that has pictures of different places in a town.

3. Find a book that tells about just one kind of job.

4. Find a book that has pictures of places that you also see in your town.

5. In which book can you find pictures of people working on machines?

6. In which book can you find pictures of people working with their hands?

7. Bring up the book that shows someone doing a job you would like to do.

WHO AM I ?

YOU'LL NEED:

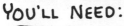

file folders

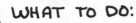

cut-outs, photos or sketches of people (showing different careers)

sewing needle

craft knife

GLUE — glue

FOLDER BACK

FOLDER FRONT

WHAT TO DO:

1. Adult glues a picture of community helper, dressed in uniform and with equipment, onto the inside back of a file folder.

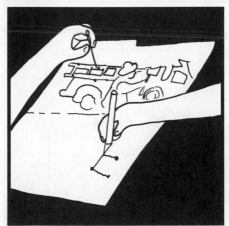

2. Fold front of folder back under glued-on picture. With the needle press four dots around parts in the picture where you want to highlight. Make sure needle points show through to front cover. Open up folder; connect 3 dots to make doors and cut open.

WHO AM I ?

2   3   4

1

3. Close folder so doors only can be seen. Place a number on each door. Start with "1" on the most difficult clue. Clue "4" is easiest and most revealing. Child opens door "1" first and guesses career.

A SPINNER GAME

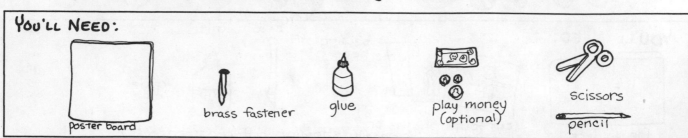

You'll Need:

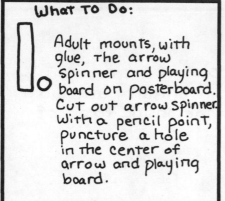

poster board

brass fastener

glue

play money (optional)

scissors

pencil

What to do:

1. Adult mounts, with glue, the arrow spinner and playing board on posterboard. Cut out arrow spinner. With a pencil point, puncture a hole in the center of arrow and playing board.

2. Place one brass fastener through arrow spinner and then through hole on playing board. Make sure spinner freely moves.

3. To play: Child spins arrow. Child names place where spinner stops and names type of person who might work there. They can describe uniforms, if any, and equipment used by person.

Variations:

★ Child gets paid—in play money—for each correct spin. If he cannot name a new person who works in that particular place—on each successive spin—he gets no play money. Winner can be player with most "pay".

★ Child can spin and tell who he/she would like to be if he/she worked in that particular place.

★ Add new pictures for new job categories

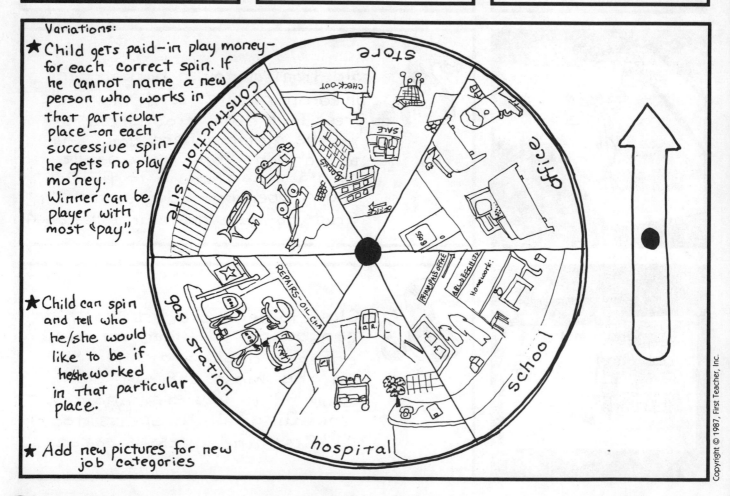

BIBLIOGRAPHY

Bate, Norman. *Who Built the Bridge?*. Crown, 1975.

Bester, Roger. *Fireman Jim*. Crown, 1981.

Bundt, Nancy. *The Fire Station Book*. Carolrhoda, 1981.

Ekker, Ernst. *What Is Beyond the Hill?*. Lippincott, 1986.

Florian, Douglas. *People Working*. Thomas Y. Crowell, 1983.

Friedman, Joy Troth. *Look Around and Listen.* , 1900.

Gibbons, Gail. *Department Store*. Thomas Y. Crowell, 1984.

_____ . *The Post Office Book*. Thomas Y. Crowell, 1984.

Greene, Carla. *Truck Drivers. What Do They Do?*. Harper & Row, 1967.

Grunsell, Angela. *At the Doctor*. Franklin Watts, 1983.

Hautzig, Deborah. *A Visit to the Sesame Street Hospital*. Random House, 1985.

Hoban, Tana. *Dig, Drill, Dump, Fill*. Greenwillow, 1975.

Isadora, Rachel. *City Seen from A to Z*. Greenwillow, 1983.

Klein, Norma. *Girls Can Be Anything*. E. P. Dutton, 1973.

Knight, Hilary. *Where's Wallace?*. Harper & Row, 1964.

LeSeig, Theo. *Maybe You Should Fly a Jet*. Random House, 1986.

Le Tord, Bijou. *Good Wood Bear*. Bradbury, 1985.

Matthais, Catherine. *I Can Be a Police Officer*. Children's Press, 1984.

Munroe, Roxie. *The Inside Outside Book of New York City*. Dodd, Mead, 1985.

Rey, Margaret. *Curious George Visits the Zoo*. Houghton Mifflin, 1985.

_____ . *Curious George at the Fire Station*. Houghton Mifflin, 1985.

Robbins, Ken. *City/Country.*. Viking/Kestrel, 1985.

Rockwell, Anne. *Fire Engines*. E. P. Dutton, 1985.

Scarry, Richard. *At Work*. Western, 1976.

Stevenson, James. *Grandpa's Great City Book*. Greenwillow, 1983.

Zolotow, Charlotte. *The Park Book*. Harper & Row, 1944.

PARTNERS FOR LEARNING

JANET HOROWITZ   KATHY FAGGELLA

NEW BOOKS from FIRST TEACHER

Partners for Learning is based on the belief that parents and teachers are partners in the education of young children. The book is a guide to the development of positive parent participation in schools—from orientation meetings and potluck parent/child meals to parent-sponsored fundraisers and parent volunteer projects. It's a must for the caring classroom!

THINK IT THROUGH

CELEBRATE EVERY DAY

BUILDING ON BOOKS

MARTHA A. HAYES   ANNE H. LEONE   KATHY FAGGELLA

Unique in its organized approach to the teaching of thinking skills to young children, this book offers a great variety of activities for each area of the classroom and curriculum. Each activity develops a specific thinking skill. In addition, there are suggestions for developing creativity and problem-solving skills.

An anthology of the best ideas for celebrations from FIRST TEACHER, this book is based on the experience of hundreds of early childhood teachers. From original ideas for traditional holidays and seasonal celebrations to birthday parties in school and multi-cultural special events, this book will show you how to teach your children that every day is worth celebrating.

A comprehensive guide to integrating children's literature into all areas of the early childhood curriculum. There are hundreds of annotated book suggestions, each with a motivating or follow-up activity.

TO ORDER:

Send $9.95 (plus $1 for each book's postage and handling) to:

First Teacher, Inc.
Box 29
60 Main St.
Bridgeport, CT 06602

OR CALL:
1-800-341-1522

Q: WHERE CAN YOU FIND HUNDREDS OF CLASSROOM TESTED IDEAS *EACH MONTH* TO HELP YOUR CHILDREN LEARN AND GROW?

A: IN FIRST TEACHER

Each 16 page issue of FIRST TEACHER provides you with innovative projects to make each day an exciting new adventure. We give you ideas for toymaking, games and recipes to do with young children. We take you to the world of make believe with ideas for drama and creative movement. And experts recommend the very best books for young children in FIRST TEACHER.

FIRST TEACHER has a newspaper format, but it's something to read and save. Each issue has a topical theme, so each one adds a permanent resource of projects and ideas to your school or center.

FIRST TEACHER is written by experienced caregivers, daycare directors, and nursery teachers, so it's full of tested ideas to help you guide and motivate young children

FIRST TEACHER has been read and used by over 30,000 Early Childhood teachers. Here's what one of them, Racelle Mednikow, preschool teacher for 16 years, says:

"What a pleasure to be provided with well written, resourceful and usable ideas that can be interjected into our everyday curriculum and be of true value to each of our teachers!"

"Thank you so much for this delightful, informative newspaper."

Subscribe today! Don't miss another month of ideas, projects, and activities.

From the authors of **CONCEPT COOKERY**

CRAYONS CRAFTS AND CONCEPTS

by

Kathy Faggella

Art activities can teach basic concepts and be integrated into the whole curriculum. Presented in one page, easy-to-read formats, that even your children can follow, these 50+ projects will fit into each theme and subject area, you introduce. There are also suggestions for setting up an art area, making smocks, safety rules, and follow ups for each activity. Projects are designed to be reproduced and sent home for follow up, too.

TABLE OF CONTENTS

TO ORDER:

Send $9.95 (plus $1 for each book's postage and handling) to:

First Teacher, Inc.
Box 29
60 Main St.
Bridgeport, CT. 06602

OR CALL: 1-800-341-1522